P9-ARI-960

Fodor's® New EDITION

Pocket
Istanbul

Excerpted from *Fodor's Turkey*

Fodor's Travel Publications, Inc.
New York • Toronto • London • Sydney • Auckland
www.fodors.com

Fodor's Pocket Istanbul

EDITORS: Natasha Lesser and Stephanie J. Adler

Editorial Contributors: David Brown, Gareth Jenkins, Christina Knight, Helayne Schiff, M. T. Schwartzman (Essential Information editor)

Editorial Production: Tom Holton

Maps: David Lindroth, *cartographer*; Steven Amsterdam, *map editor*

Design: Fabrizio La Rocca, *creative director*; Guido Caroti, *associate art director*; Lyndell Brookhouse-Gil, *cover design*; Jolie Novak, *photo editor*

Production/Manufacturing: Mike Costa

Cover Photograph: Owen Franken

Copyright

First Edition

ISBN 0–679–00291–X

Special Sales

Fodor's Travel Publications are available at special discounts for bulk purchases for sales promotions or premiums. Special editions, including personalized covers, excerpts of existing guides, and corporate imprints, can be created in large quantities for special needs. For more information, contact your local bookseller or write to Special Markets, Fodor's Travel Publications, 201 East 50th Street, New York, NY 10022. Inquiries from Canada should be directed to your local Canadian bookseller or sent to Random House of Canada, Ltd., Marketing Department, 2775 Matheson Boulevard East, Mississauga, Ontario L4W 4P7. Inquiries from the United Kingdom should be sent to Fodor's Travel Publications, 20 Vauxhall Bridge Road, London SW1V 2SA, England.

CONTENTS

Maps

ON THE ROAD WITH FODOR'S

WHEN I PLAN A VA-CATION, the first thing I do is cast around among my friends and colleagues to find someone who's just been where I'm going. That's because there's no substitute for a recommendation from a good friend who knows your tastes, your budget, and your circumstances, someone who's just been there. Unfortunately, such friends are few and far between. So it's nice to know that there's *Fodor's Pocket Istanbul*.

In the first place, this book won't stay home when you hit the road. It will accompany you every step of the way, steering you away from wrong turns and wrong choices and never expecting a thing in return. Most important of all, it's written and assiduously updated by the kind of people you *would* hit up for travel tips if you knew them. They're as choosy as your pickiest friend, and they're equipped with an insider's knowledge of Istanbul. In these pages, they don't send you chasing down every town and sight in Istanbul but have instead selected the best ones, the ones that are worthy of your time and money. Will this be the vacation of your dreams? We hope so.

About Our Writers

Our success in helping to make your trip the best of all possible vacations is a credit to the hard work of our extraordinary writers.

Gareth Jenkins, who updated all of the material in this book, has a degree in Ancient Greek and Latin from Durham University, England. After graduating, Gareth worked as an archaeologist and writer in the United Kingdom before setting off to travel and teach English in the Mediterranean. He spent five years in Egypt, Greece, and Israel before moving to Istanbul, where he has lived since 1989. He works as a freelance journalist, writer, translator, and editor. He has published two books on Turkey and is researching a third on Turkish politics.

Fodor's Turkey editor **Natasha Lesser,** who visited Turkey for the first time in October 1998, fell in love with the bustling streets of Istanbul and the turquoise waters along the Mediterranean and Aegean. Though she has traveled all over the world, she found Turkey to be one of the most enchanting places she has ever visited.

We'd also like to thank Erbil Gunasti at the Turkish Mission to

the United Nations and Delta Airlines for assisting us with research.

Connections

We're pleased that the American Society of Travel Agents continues to endorse Fodor's as its guidebook of choice. ASTA is the world's largest and most influential travel trade association, operating in more than 170 countries, with 27,000 members pledged to adhere to a strict code of ethics reflecting the Society's motto, "Integrity in Travel." ASTA shares Fodor's devotion to providing smart, honest travel information and advice to travelers, and we've long recommended that our readers—even those who have guidebooks and traveling friends—consult ASTA member agents for the experience and professionalism they bring to your vacation planning.

On Fodor's Web site (www.fodors.com), check out the Resource Center, an on-line companion to the Essential Information section of this book, complete with useful hot links to related sites. In our forums, you can also get lively advice from other travelers and more great tips from Fodor's experts worldwide.

How to Use This Book

Organization

Up front is **Essential Information,** an easy-to-use section arranged alphabetically by topic. Under each listing you'll find tips and information that will help you accomplish what you need to in Istanbul. You'll also find addresses and telephone numbers of organizations and companies that offer destination-related services and detailed information and publications.

The first chapter in the guide, **Destination: Istanbul,** helps get you in the mood for your trip. Pleasures and Pastimes describes the activities and sights that make Istanbul unique, and Quick Tours lays out a selection of half-day itineraries that will help you make the most of your time in Istanbul.

The **Exploring Istanbul** chapter is divided into five neighborhoods. Each lists sights alphabetically and has a suggested walk that will take you around to the major sights.

The remaining chapters are arranged in alphabetical order by subject—**Dining, Lodging, Nightlife and the Arts, Shopping,** and **Side Trips from Istanbul.**

Icons and Symbols
★ Our special recommendations
✕ Restaurant
🏠 Lodging establishment
🐣 Good for kids (rubber duck)
☞ Sends you to another section of the guide for more information
✉ Address
☎ Telephone number
☉ Opening and closing times

📷 Admission prices (those we give apply to adults; substantially reduced fees are almost always available for children, students, and senior citizens)

Numbers in white and black circles (e.g., ③ ❸) that appear on the maps, in the margins, and within the tours correspond to one another.

Dining and Lodging

The restaurants and lodgings we list are the cream of the crop in each price range.

Prices in the restaurant chart below are per person and include an appetizer, main course, and dessert but not drinks and gratuities. A service charge of 10% to 15% is added to the bill; waiters expect another 10%. If a restaurant's menu has no prices listed, ask before you order—you'll avoid a surprise when the bill comes.

CATEGORY	ISTANBUL	SIDE TRIPS
$$$$	over $40	over $30
$$$	$25–$40	$20–$30
$$	$12–$25	$10–$20
$	under $12	under $10

Prices in the lodging chart below are for two people in a double room, including VAT and service charge.

CATEGORY	ISTANBUL	SIDE TRIPS
$$$$	over $200	over $150
$$$	$100–$200	$100–$150
$$	$60–$100	$50–$100
$	under $60	under $50

Hotel Facilities

We always list the facilities that are available—but we don't specify whether you'll be charged extra to use them: When pricing accommodations, always ask what's included. In addition, assume that all rooms have private baths unless noted otherwise. In addition, when you book a room, be sure to mention if you have a disability or are traveling with children, if you prefer a private bath or a certain type of bed, or if you have specific dietary needs or other concerns.

Assume that hotels operate on the **European Plan** (EP, with no meals) unless we specify that they include breakfast or other meals in the rates.

Restaurant Reservations and Dress Codes

Reservations are always a good idea; we mention them only when they are essential or not accepted. Book as far ahead as you can, and reconfirm as soon as you arrive. Unless otherwise noted, the restaurants listed are open daily for lunch and dinner. We mention dress only when men are required to wear a jacket or a jacket and tie. Look for an overview of local dining habits in the Pleasures and Pastimes section of Chapter 1 and in Chapter 3.

Credit Cards

The following abbreviations are used: **AE**, American Express; **DC**, Diners Club; **MC**, MasterCard; and **V**, Visa.

Don't Forget to Write

You can use this book in the confidence that all prices and opening times are based on information supplied to us at press time; Fodor's cannot accept responsibility for any errors. Time inevitably brings changes, so always confirm information when it matters—especially if you're making a detour to visit a specific place.

Were the restaurants we recommended as described? Did our hotel picks exceed your expectations? Did you find a museum we recommended a waste of time? Keeping a travel guide fresh and up-to-date is a big job, and we welcome your feedback, positive *and* negative. If you have complaints, we'll look into them and revise our entries when the facts warrant it. If you've discovered a special place that we haven't included, we'll pass the information along to our correspondents and have them check it out. So send us your thoughts via e-mail at editors@fodors.com (specifying the name of the book on the subject line) or on paper in care of the Turkey editor at Fodor's, 201 East 50th Street, New York, New York 10022. In the meantime, have a wonderful trip!

Karen Cure
Editorial Director

Istanbul

HALICIOĞLU

HASKÖY

KULAKSIZ
MEZARLIĞI

KASIMPAŞA

TO
EDIRNE

AYVANSARAY

BALAT

FENER

EDIRNEKAPI

Haliç (Golden Horn)

UNKAPANI

GALATA

KÜÇÜKPAZAR

EMINÖ
Sirkeci
Station

SIRKECI

CAĞALOĞLU

BEYAZIT

SULTANA

KUMKAPI

Kennedy Cad.

Kennedy Cad.

| 0 | | 440 yards |
| 0 | | 400 meters |

KEY

ℹ Tourist Information

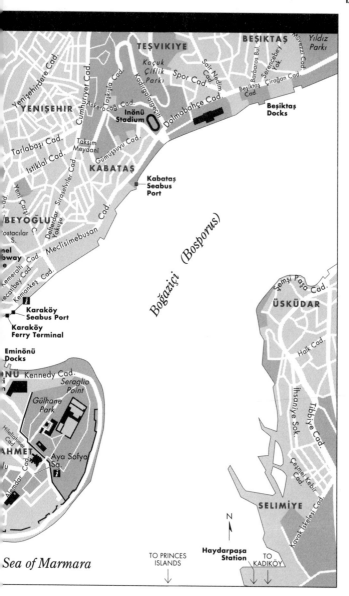

Europe

Reykjavík
ICELAND

NORWAY

Bergen

SCOTLAND

NORTHERN
IRELAND

Edinburgh

*North
Sea*

Skagerrak

Belfast

IRELAND
*Irish
Sea*

Dublin

UNITED
KINGDOM

DENMARK

WALES

Cardiff

ENGLAND

NETHERLANDS

Hamburg

London

The Hague

Amsterdam

English Channel

Rotterdam

GERMA

*ATLANTIC
OCEAN*

Brussels

BELGIUM

Bonn

Paris

LUXEMBOURG

Frankfurt

FRANCE

Zürich

Munich

Bern
SWITZERLAND

Lyon

LIECHTENSTEIN

Ljub

Milan

Venice

PORTUGAL

Madrid

ANDORRA

Marseille

Nice

Monte
Carlo
MONACO

Florence

Lisbon

Barcelona

Corsica

SPAIN

Seville

Granada

*Balearic
Islands*

Sardinia

Tyrrhenian

Gibraltar

Mediterranean Sea

MOROCCO

ALGERIA

400 miles

TUNISIA

0

600 km

ESSENTIAL INFORMATION

Basic Information on Traveling in Istanbul, Savvy Tips to Make Your Trip a Breeze, and Companies and Organizations to Contact

AIR TRAVEL

Turkey's major airport is Istanbul's **Atatürk Airport**, about 18 km (12 mi) from the city. Try to arrive at the airport at least 45 minutes before takeoff because security checks at the entrance to the terminal can be time-consuming; **checked luggage must be identified by boarding passengers before it is put on the plane,** and all unidentified luggage is left behind and checked for bombs or firearms.

Flying time is 11 hours from New York, 13 hours from Chicago, and 15 hours from Los Angeles. The flight from Toronto to Istanbul takes 11½ hours. Flying time from London is 4 hours.

➤ AIRPORT INFORMATION: **Atatürk Airport** (☎ 212/663–6400).

CARRIERS

When flying internationally, you must usually choose between a domestic carrier, the national flag carrier of the country you are visiting, and a foreign carrier from a third country. You may, for example, choose to fly THY/Turkish Airlines to Turkey. National flag carriers have the greatest number of nonstops. Domestic carriers may have better connections to your home town and serve a greater number of gateway cities. Third-party carriers may have a price advantage.

➤ MAJOR AIRLINES: From the U.S.: **Air Canada** (☎ 800/776–3000). **Air France** (☎ 800/237–2747). **British Airways** (☎ 800/247–9297). **Delta** (☎ 800/241–4141). **Lufthansa** (☎ 800/645–3880). **Northwest/KLM** (☎ 800/447–4747). **Olympic Airlines** (☎ 800/223–1226). **Swissair** (☎ 800/221–4750). **TWA** (☎ 800/221–2000 in the U.S. or ☎ 800/892–4141). **THY/Turkish Airlines** (☎ 212/339–9650 or 800/874–8875; ☎ 212/663–6300 in Istanbul or, for reservations, ☎ 212/663–6363), the Turkish national airline. From Canada: **Air Canada** (☎ 800/776–3000). **British Airways** (☎ 800/247–9297). **Air France** (☎ 800/237–2747). **Alitalia** (☎ 800/223–5730). **Finnair** (☎ 800/950–5000). **KLM** (☎ 800/374–7747). **Lufthansa** (☎ 800/645–3880). **Olympic Air** (☎ 800/223–1226). **SAS** (☎ 800/221–2350). **Swissair** (☎ 800/

221–4750). **TWA** (☎ 800/221–2000 or 800/892–4141).

➤ FROM THE U.K.: **British Airways** (☎ 0181/897–4000 or 0345/222–111 outside London) and **Turkish Airlines** (✉ 11–12 Hanover St., London W1R 9HF, ☎ 0171/499–9249 or 0171/499–4499) fly to Istanbul. **Lufthansa** (☎ 0345/737–747) flies from London to Istanbul via Frankfurt.

➤ WITHIN TURKEY: **Istanbul Airlines** (☎ 212/231–7526). **Turkish Airlines** (THY, ☎ 212/663–6300; 212/663–6363 for reservations).

TRANSFERS

Shuttle buses make the 30- to 40-minute trip from the airport's international and domestic terminals—which are some distance apart—to the Turkish Airlines office in Taksim Square; buses to the airport depart from Taksim Square every hour from 6 AM until 11 PM and as demand warrants after that. Allow at least 45 minutes for the bus ride in this direction and plan to be at the airport two hours before international flights to allow for the time-consuming security and check-in procedures.

Taxis, which are metered, charge about $15 to Taksim Square and $11 to Sultanahmet Square. For more about taxi travel in Istanbul, *see* Public Transportation, *below.*

➤ INFORMATION: **Shuttle Bus Information** (☎ 212/252–1106).

BUS TRAVEL

For information on bus travel within Istanbul, *see* Public Transportation, *below.*

Buses arrive at the Esenler Otogar, outside the city near Bayrampaşa. This terminal is accessible by the Hızlı Tren (rapid train) system, which leaves from Aksaray. However, the train is often very crowded, particularly at rush hour, and you might be better off taking a taxi. A few buses from Anatolia arrive at the Harem Terminal, on the Asian side of the Bosporus.

Most bus companies have minibus services from the bus terminals to the area around Taksim Square and Aksaray, which is close to many hotels. Private taxis cost about $12 from Esenler Terminal to Taksim or Sultanahmet and about $10 from the Harem Terminal. Note that you'll have to pay the Bosporus Bridge toll when crossing from Asia to Europe, or vice versa.

➤ INFORMATION: **Esenler Otogar** (Esenler Station; ☎ 212/658–0036). **Harem Terminal** (☎ 216/333–3763).

BUSINESS HOURS

Banks are normally open weekdays from 8:30 until noon or 12:30, depending on the bank, and from 1:30 until 5. However, selected branches of some Turkish banks now remain open during the middle of the day and for a few hours on Saturdays.

Museums are generally open Tuesday through Sunday from 9:30 until 5 or 5:30 and closed on Monday. Palaces are open the same hours but are generally closed Thursday.

Shops and bazaars are usually open Monday through Saturday from 9:30 to 1 and from 2 to 7, and closed all day on Sunday.

CAMERAS & COMPUTERS

EQUIPMENT PRECAUTIONS

Always **keep your film, tape, or computer disks out of the sun.** Carry an extra supply of batteries, and **be prepared to turn on your camera, camcorder, or laptop** to prove to security personnel that the device is real. Always **ask for hand inspection of film,** which becomes clouded after successive exposure to airport X-ray machines, and **keep videotapes and computer disks away from metal detectors.** Use an adapter and converter with your laptop (☞ Electricity, *below*).

ONLINE ON THE ROAD

Many of the better hotels have some means for guests to get online access; ask when you make a reservation. In addition, larger post offices may have connection facilities. You may also be able to find Internet cafés. Make sure to **contact your Internet-service provider before you go** to find out if it has an access number in Turkey.

CAR RENTAL

Rates in Istanbul begin at $35 a day and $250 a week for an economy car with unlimited mileage. Gas costs about 75¢ per liter. The majority of rental cars are stick shift, though it is possible to get an automatic transmission with advance arrangements.

For information about driving in Istanbul, *see* Car Travel, *below*.

➤ Major Agencies: **Avis** (☎ 800/331–1084, 800/879–2847 in Canada, 008/225–533 in Australia). **Budget** (☎ 800/527–0700, 0800/181181 in the U.K.). **Dollar** (☎ 800/800–4000, 0990/565656 in the U.K., where it is known as Eurodollar). **Hertz** (☎ 800/654–3001, 800/263–0600 in Canada, 0345/555888 in the U.K., 03/9222–2523 in Australia, 03/358–6777 in New Zealand). **National InterRent** (☎ 800/227–3876, 0345/222525 in the U.K., where it is known as Europcar InterRent).

INSURANCE

When driving a rented car you are generally responsible for any damage to or loss of the vehicle. You may also be liable for any property damage or personal injury that you may cause while driving. Before you rent and buy additional coverage, **see what coverage you already have** and check whether Turkey is covered under the terms of your personal auto-insurance policy and credit cards.

REQUIREMENTS

In Turkey **your own driver's license is acceptable.** If you have any doubts or will be staying for a long period of time, consider obtaining an International Driver's Permit from the American or Canadian automobile association, and, in the United Kingdom, from the Automobile Association or Royal Automobile Club. These international permits are universally recognized, and having one in your wallet may save you a problem with the local authorities.

SURCHARGES

Before you pick up a car in one city and leave it in another, **ask about drop-off charges or one-way service fees,** which can be substantial. To avoid a hefty refueling fee, **fill the tank just before you turn in the car,** but be aware that gas stations near the rental outlet may overcharge.

CAR TRAVEL

Turkey has one of the world's highest auto accident rates, and driving in Istanbul is generally best avoided. That said, having a car allows you freedom that traveling by bus, train, or plane does not. E80 runs between Istanbul and central Anatolia to the east; this toll road is the best of several alternatives. You can also enter or leave the city on one of the numerous car ferries that ply the Sea of Marmara from the Kabataş docks. There's an overnight ferry to İzmir from the Eminönü docks. To get out of the city by car, your best bet is to buy a map, as the signs aren't always so clear.

AUTO CLUBS

➤ CONTACT INFORMATION: **Australian Automobile Association** (☎ 06/247–7311). **Canadian Automobile Association** (CAA, ☎ 613/247–0117). **New Zealand Automobile Association** (☎ 09/377–4660). The **Türkiye Turing Ve Otomobil Kurumu** (✉ TTÖK, or Touring and Automobile Club; Şişli Halâskar Gazi Cad. 364, Istanbul, ☎ 212/231–4631) has information about driving in Turkey and does repairs. U.K.: **Automobile Association** (AA, ☎ 0990/500–600); **Royal Automobile Club** (RAC, ☎ 0990/722–722 for membership, 0345/121–345 for insurance). U.S.: **American Automobile Association** (☎ 800/564–6222).

EMERGENCY SERVICES

A road rescue service is available on some highways; **before you embark on a journey, ask your car rental agency or hotel how to contact it in case of an emergency.** Most of the major manufacturers in Turkey (for example, Renault, Fiat, and Opel/General Motors) also have roaming 24-hour services.

Most Turkish gas stations have at least one member of staff with some knowledge of car mechanics who can diagnose problems and provide "first aid" or advice, such as directions to the nearest mechanic. If a gas station attendant fixes a minor problem it is customary to give him a small tip of about 5–10 dollars depending on the time and effort expended.

In Istanbul, entire streets are given over to car-repair shops run by teams of experts—one specializes in radiators, another in electrical fittings, and another in steering columns. It's not expensive to have repairs done, but it's customary to give a small tip to the person who did the repairs. If you don't want to wait at the shop for the work to be done, **take all car documents with you when you leave the shop.**

GASOLINE
Shell, British Petroleum, Total, Elf, and two Turkish oil companies, Petrol Ofisi and Türkpetrol, operate stations in Turkey. Those on the main highways stay open around the clock, others from 6 AM to 10 PM.

ROAD CONDITIONS
Signposts are few, lighting scarce, and city traffic chaotic, and the country's accident rate is one of the highest in Europe. Urban streets and highways are jammed with vehicles operated by high-speed lunatics and drivers who constantly honk their horns. In Istanbul, it's safer and faster to drive on the modern highways. Avoid the many small one-way streets—you never know when someone is going to barrel down one of them in the wrong direction. Better yet, leave your car in a garage and use public transportation or take taxis.

RULES OF THE ROAD
In general, Turkish driving conforms to Mediterranean customs, with driving on the right and passing on the left. Be prepared for drivers to do anything. Seatbelts are required for front seat passengers, and a good idea for those in the back seats. Using a cellular phone while driving is prohibited.

CUSTOMS & DUTIES
When shopping, **keep receipts** for all of your purchases. Upon reentering your home country, **be ready to show customs officials what you've bought.** If you feel a duty is incorrect, appeal the assessment. If you object to the way your clearance was handled, get the inspector's badge number. In either case, first ask to see a supervisor, then write to the appropriate authorities, beginning with the port director at your point of entry.

IN TURKEY
Turkish customs officials rarely look through tourists' luggage on arrival. You are allowed to bring in 400 cigarettes, 50 cigars, 200 grams of tobacco, 1½ kilograms of instant coffee, 500 grams of tea, and 2½ liters of alcohol. Register all valuable personal items in your passport at your embassy on entry. Items in the duty-free shops

in Turkish airports, for international arrivals, are usually less expensive here than in European airports or in flight.

IN AUSTRALIA

Australia residents who are 18 or older may bring back A$400 worth of souvenirs and gifts (including jewelry), 250 cigarettes or 250 grams of tobacco, and 1,125 ml of alcohol (including wine, beer, and spirits). Residents under 18 may bring back A$200 worth of goods.

➤ INFORMATION: **Australian Customs Service** (Regional Director, ✉ Box 8, Sydney, NSW 2001, ☎ 02/9213–2000, FAX 02/9213–4000).

IN CANADA

Canadian residents who have been out of Canada for at least 7 days may bring in C$500 worth of goods duty-free. If you've been away less than 7 days but more than 48 hours, the duty-free allowance drops to C$200; if your trip lasts 24 to 48 hours, the allowance is C$50. You may not pool allowances with family members. Goods claimed under the C$500 exemption may follow you by mail; those claimed under the lesser exemptions must accompany you. Alcohol and tobacco products may be included in the 7-day and 48-hour exemptions but not in the 24-hour exemption. If you meet the age requirements of the province or territory through

which you reenter Canada, you may bring in, duty-free, 1.14 liters (40 imperial ounces) of wine or liquor *or* 24 12-ounce cans or bottles of beer or ale. If you are 16 or older you may bring in, duty-free, 200 cigarettes and 50 cigars.

You may send an unlimited number of gifts worth up to C$60 each duty-free to Canada. Label the package UNSOLICITED GIFT—VALUE UNDER $60. Alcohol and tobacco are excluded.

➤ INFORMATION: **Revenue Canada** (✉ 2265 St. Laurent Blvd. S, Ottawa, Ontario K1G 4K3, ☎ 613/993–0534, 800/461–9999 in Canada).

IN NEW ZEALAND

Homeward-bound residents with goods to declare must present themselves for inspection. If you're 17 or older, you may bring back $700 worth of souvenirs and gifts. Your duty-free allowance also includes 4.5 liters of wine or beer; one 1,125-ml bottle of spirits; and either 200 cigarettes, 250 grams of tobacco, 50 cigars, or a combo of all three up to 250 grams.

➤ INFORMATION: **New Zealand Customs** (✉ Custom House, 50 Anzac Ave., Box 29, Auckland, New Zealand, ☎ 09/359–6655, 09/309–2978).

IN THE U.K.

From countries outside the EU, including Turkey, you may import, duty-free, 200 cigarettes or 50 cigars; 1 liter of spirits or 2 liters of fortified or sparkling wine or liqueurs; 2 liters of still table wine; 60 milliliters of perfume; 250 milliliters of toilet water; plus £136 worth of other goods, including gifts and souvenirs.

➤ INFORMATION: **HM Customs and Excise** (✉ Dorset House, Stamford St., London SE1 9NG, ☎ 0171/202–4227).

IN THE U.S.

U.S. residents may bring home $400 worth of foreign goods duty-free if they've been out of the country for at least 48 hours (and if they haven't used the $400 allowance or any part of it in the past 30 days).

U.S. residents 21 and older may bring back 1 liter of alcohol duty-free. In addition, regardless of your age, you are allowed 200 cigarettes and 100 non-Cuban cigars. Antiques, which the U.S. Customs Service defines as objects more than 100 years old, enter duty-free, as do original works of art done entirely by hand, including paintings, drawings, and sculptures.

You may also send packages home duty-free: up to $200 worth of goods for personal use, with a limit of one parcel per addressee per day (and no alcohol or tobacco products or perfume worth more than $5); label the package PERSONAL USE, and attach a list of its contents and their retail value. Do

not label the package UNSOLICITED GIFT, or your duty-free exemption will drop to $100. Mailed items do not affect your duty-free allowance on your return.

➤ INFORMATION: **U.S. Customs Service** (Inquiries, ✉ Box 7407, Washington, DC 20044, ☎ 202/927–6724; complaints, ✉ Office of Regulations and Rulings, 1301 Constitution Ave. NW, Washington, DC 20229; registration of equipment, ✉ Resource Management, 1301 Constitution Ave. NW, Washington, DC 20229, ☎ 202/927–0540).

DINING

Lunch is generally served from noon to 3, dinner from 7 to 10. You can find restaurants or cafés open almost any time of the day or night in cities; in villages, getting a meal at odd hours can be a problem. Breakfast starts early, typically by 7 AM.

Except for at restaurants classified as $$$$, where a jacket and tie are usually appropriate, you can get by in jeans and sneakers.

For more information on dining in Istanbul, *see* Pleasures and Pastimes in Chapter 1, and Chapter 3.

PRECAUTIONS

Tap water is heavily chlorinated and supposedly safe to drink. It's best to play it safe, however, and stick to *şişe suyu* (bottled still water), *maden suyu* (bottled, sparkling mineral water), or *maden sodası* (carbonated mineral water), which are better-tasting and inexpensive. Otherwise, Turkish food is relatively safe.

DISABILITIES & ACCESSIBILITY

ACCESS IN TURKEY

Unfortunately, Turkey isn't on par with other parts of the world in terms of accessibility. However, many city buses have special seats designated for passengers with disabilities, and some "kneel" to make it easier for less-mobile travelers to board. Though some museums and upscale hotels have ramps and elevators, you are less likely to find these in older museums and small pensions. But locals are likely to be very helpful.

DISCOUNTS & DEALS

CREDIT-CARD BENEFITS

When you use your credit card to make travel purchases you may get free travel-accident insurance, collision-damage insurance, and medical or legal assistance, depending on the card and the bank that issued it. American Express, MasterCard, and Visa provide one or more of these services, so **get a copy of your credit card's travel-benefits policy.**

DISCOUNT RESERVATIONS

➤ AIRLINE TICKETS: ☎ 800/FLY–4–LESS.

➤ HOTEL ROOMS: **Hotels Plus** (☎ 800/235–0909). **International Marketing & Travel Concepts** (☎ 800/790–4682). **Steigenberger Reservation Service** (☎ 800/223–5652). **Travel Interlink** (☎ 800/888–5898).

ELECTRICITY

To use your U.S.-purchased electric-powered equipment, **bring a converter and adapter.** The electrical current in Turkey is 220 volts, 50 cycles alternating current (AC); wall outlets take Continental-type plugs, with two or three round prongs.

If your appliances are dual-voltage, you'll need only an adapter. Don't use 110-volt outlets, marked FOR SHAVERS ONLY, for high-wattage appliances such as blow-dryers. Most laptops operate equally well on 110 and 220 volts and so require only an adapter.

EMBASSIES AND CONSULATES

If you have lost your passport or are in need of other assistance, contact your country's embassy or consulate.

➤ CONTACT INFORMATION: **Australia** (⊠ 58 Tepecik Yolu, Etiler, ☎ 212/257–7050). **Canada** (⊠ 107/3 Büyükdere Cad., Gayrettepe, ☎ 212/272–5174). **New Zealand** (⊠ 13/4 Iran Cad., Kavaklıdere, Ankara, ☎ 312/467–9056). **U.K.** (⊠ 34 Meşrutiyet Cad., Tepebaşı, ☎ 212/293–7540). **U.S.** (⊠ 104 Meşrutiyet Cad., Tepebaşı, ☎ 212/251–3602).

EMERGENCIES

If your passport is lost or stolen, contact the police and your embassy immediately (☞ Embassies and Consulates, *above*). For information about food and staying healthy, *see* Dining, *above,* and Health, *below*.

➤ EMERGENCY CONTACTS: **Ambulance** (☎ 112). **Emergency** (police, etc.; ☎ 155). **Tourism Police** (Istanbul; ☎ 212/527–4503).

➤ LATE-NIGHT PHARMACIES: Information is available about **24-hour pharmacies** (☎ 111); note that operators generally don't speak English. There's a pharmacy in every neighborhood, and all Istanbul pharmacies post the name and address of the nearest one open around the clock. The names of 24-hour pharmacies are also available through the **directory inquiries service** (☎ 118), although it is advisable to ask a Turkish speaker to make the call. **Taksim** (⊠ İstiklal Cad. 17, ☎ 212/244–3195), one good pharmacy, is centrally located in the Taksim district.

ENGLISH-LANGUAGE BOOKSTORES

See Chapter 6 for information about English-language bookstores in Istanbul.

ETIQUETTE & BEHAVIOR

MOSQUES

Turkey is comparatively lenient regarding the visiting of mosques—in many Muslim countries, non-Muslims are strictly forbidden to enter them at all. Most mosques in Turkey are open to the public during the day. Prayer sessions, called *namaz,* last 30 to 40 minutes and are observed five times daily. These times are based on the position of the sun, so they vary throughout the seasons but are generally around sunrise (between 5 and 7), at lunchtime (around noon or 1, when the sun is directly overhead), in the afternoon (around 3 or 4), at sunset (usually between 5 and 7), and at bedtime (at 9 or 10). (A daily list of prayer times can be found in Turkish newspapers.) During *namaz,* it's best not to enter a mosque. Non-Muslims should especially **avoid visiting mosques at midday on Friday**, when Muslims are required to congregate and worship.

For women, **bare arms and legs are not acceptable inside a mosque.** Men should avoid wearing shorts as well. Women should not enter a mosque without first covering their heads with a scarf, though some guardians will overlook it when a female tourist does not cover her head.

Before entering a mosque, **shoes must be removed.** There is usually an attendant, and shoes are generally safe. If you feel uncomfortable about leaving them you can always carry them in your backpack or handbag. It is considered offensive for a non-Muslim to sit down in a mosque (many tourists do sit down despite the signs requesting them not to).

A small donation is usually requested for the upkeep of the mosque. Approximately 50¢ to $1 U.S. is appropriate. Some mosques heavily visited by tourists may also have a "shoekeeper," who will ask for a tip. You should not feel obliged to give him any money.

HEALTH

No serious health risks are associated with travel to Turkey. No vaccinations are required for entry. However, to avoid problems at customs, diabetics carrying needles and syringes should have a letter from their physician confirming their need for insulin injections. Rabies can be a problem in Turkey, even occasionally in Istanbul. If bitten or scratched by a dog or cat about which you have suspicions, go to the nearest pharmacy and ask for assistance.

For minor problems, **pharmacists can be helpful,** and medical services are widely available. Doctors and dentists abound in Istanbul; many are women. There are also *hastane* (hospitals) and *klinik* (clinics).

For information about health and food, *see* Dining, *above;* for emergency-contact numbers and medical resources, *see* Emergencies, *above.*

HOLIDAYS

January 1 (New Year's Day); January 19–21 (Şeker Bayramı, marking the end of Ramadan); March 29–31 (Kurban Bayramı, an important religious holiday, honoring Abraham's willingness to sacrifice his son to God); April 23 (National Independence Day); May 19 (Atatürk's Commemoration Day, celebrating his birthday and the day he landed in Samsun, starting the independence movement); August 30 (Zafer Bayramı, or Victory Day, commemorating Turkish victories over Greek forces in 1922, during Turkey's War of Independence); October 29 (Cumhuriyet Bayramı, or Republic Day, celebrating Atatürk's proclamation of the Turkish republic in 1923); November 10 (the anniversary of Atatürk's death, commemorated most notably by a nationwide moment of silence at 9:05 AM).

Please bear in mind that **Muslim religious holidays are based on the lunar calendar and shift about 10 days backwards each year.** The dates given here for the Şeker and Kurban holidays are for 1999. In 2000 the dates for the Şeker Bayramı and Kurban Bayramı will be January 9–11 and March 18–21 respectively.

LANGUAGE

In 1928, Atatürk launched sweeping language reforms that, over a period of six weeks, replaced Arabic script with the Latin-based alphabet and eliminated many Arabic and Persian words from the Turkish language.

English, German, and sometimes French are widely spoken in hotels, restaurants, and shops. Try learning a few basic Turkish words, it will be appreciated.

LODGING

Accommodations range from international luxury chain hotels to charming inns occupying historic Ottoman mansions and caravansaries. It's advisable to **plan ahead for the peak season (from April to October).**

Note that **reservations should be confirmed more than once.** Phone reservations are not always honored, so it's a good idea to fax the hotel and get a written confirmation of your reservations, as well as to call again before you arrive. If you want air-conditioning, make sure to ask about it when you reserve.

Asking to see the room in advance is accepted practice. It will probably be much more basic than the well-decorated reception area. Check for noise, especially if the room faces a street or is anywhere near a nightclub or disco, and look for such amenities as window screens and mosquito coils—small, flat disks that, when lighted, emit an unscented vapor that keeps biting insects away.

For more information, *see* Pleasures and Pastimes in Chapter 1, and Chapter 4.

MAIL

POSTAL RATES

Rates are frequently adjusted to keep pace with inflation, but the cost of sending a letter or postcard remains nominal. Shipping a 10-pound rug home via surface mail will cost about $25 and take from two to six months.

POST OFFICES

Post offices are painted bright yellow and have PTT (Post, Telegraph, and Telephone) signs on the front. The central POs in larger cities are open Monday through Saturday from 8 AM to 9 PM, Sunday from 9 to 7. Smaller ones are open Monday through Saturday between 8:30 and 5.

RECEIVING MAIL

If you're uncertain where you'll be staying, have mail sent to Poste Restante, *Merkez Posthanesi* (Central Post Office).

MONEY

The monetary unit is the Turkish lira (TL), which comes in bank notes of 50,000; 100,000; 500,000; 1,000,000; and 5,000,000. Smaller denominations come in coins of 5,000; 10,000; 25,000; and 50,000. In mid-December 1998, the exchange rate was TL 310,000 to the U.S. dollar, TL 199,984 to the Canadian dollar, and TL 521,816 to the pound sterling.

Note that Turks often quote prices minus the last three zeros, or even the last five or six zeros. For 250,000,000 TL, for instance, a shopkeeper will say *iki büçük* (two and a half) or will mark the price tag 2,500 TL.

COSTS

Turkey is the least expensive of the Mediterranean countries. Although inflation hovers between 70% and 100%, frequent devaluations of the lira keep prices fairly stable against foreign currencies (which is why prices in this guide are listed in U.S. dollars). Only at top establishments in Istanbul do costs approach those in Europe.

Coffee can range from about 30¢ to $2.50 a cup, depending on whether it's the less expensive Turkish coffee or American-style coffee and whether it's served in a luxury hotel or a café; tea, 20¢– $2 a glass; local beer, $1–$3; soft drinks, $1–$3; lamb shish kebab, $1.50–$7; taxi, $1 for 1 km (50% higher between midnight and 6 AM).

CREDIT & DEBIT CARDS & ATMS

Credit cards—primarily Visa and MasterCard, and sometimes American Express or Diners Club—are readily accepted in Istanbul. Note, however, that many budget-oriented restaurants or hotels do not accept credit cards.

ATMs can be found throughout the city. Many accept international credit cards or bank cards (a strip of logos is usually displayed above the ATM). Almost all ATMs have a language key that enables you to read the instructions in English. For you to use your card in Turkey, your PIN must be four digits long.

Using an ATM is one of the easiest ways to get money in Turkey. Generally the exchange rate is based on the Turkish Central Bank or the exchange rate according to your bank. The exchange rate is almost always better through an ATM than with traveler's checks, but not as good as when exchanging cash.

If you're planning to get a cash advance on your credit card while in Turkey, it's a good idea to inform the credit company as companies have been known to put freezes on credit cards because they have assumed that transactions in Turkey were fraudulent.

➤ ATM LOCATIONS: **Cirrus** (☎ 800/424–7787). **Plus** (☎ 800/ 843–7587) for locations in the U.S. and Canada, or visit your local bank.

➤ REPORTING LOST CARDS: **American Express** (☎ collect, 336/393– 1111). **Diner's Club** (☎ collect, 303/799–1504). **MasterCard** (☎ toll free, 0080013/887–0903).

EXCHANGING MONEY

Because Turkey constantly devalues its currency, wait to change money until you arrive. To avoid lines at airport exchange booths, however, **get a bit of local currency before you leave home.**

If you are staying for more than a few days, do not change all your money as soon as you arrive, as the exchange rate changes every day. Your best bet is to **shop around the exchange booths for the best rate and change enough only for the next few days.** A growing number of privately operated exchange booths offer significantly better rates than hotels or banks. Paying in American dollars, too, can sometimes lead to an extra discount on your purchase.

Although fees charged for ATM transactions may be higher abroad than at home, Cirrus and Plus exchange rates are excellent, because they are based on wholesale rates offered only by major banks. You won't do as well at exchange booths in airports or rail and bus stations, in hotels, in restaurants, or in stores, although you may find their hours more convenient.

➤ EXCHANGE SERVICES: **Chase Currency To Go** (☎ 800/935–9935; 935–9935 in NY, NJ, and CT). **International Currency Express** (☎ 888/842–0880 on the East Coast of the U.S., 888/278–6628 on the West Coast). **Thomas Cook Currency Services** (☎ 800/287–7362 for telephone orders and retail locations).

TRAVELER'S CHECKS

Many places in Istanbul do not take traveler's checks, and even those that do invariably offer better exchange rates for cash. Lost or stolen checks, however, can usually be replaced within 24 hours, so you may want the added security of traveler's checks even if they prove a little more expensive. To ensure a speedy refund, buy your own traveler's checks—don't let someone else pay for them: irregularities like this can cause delays. The person who bought the checks should make the call to request a refund.

PASSPORTS & VISAS

When traveling internationally, **carry a passport** (it's always the best form of identification, which you are required to carry at all times in Turkey), and make **two photocopies of the data page** (one for someone at home and another for you, carried separately from your passport). If you lose your passport, promptly call the nearest embassy or consulate and the local police.

ENTERING TURKEY

➤ AUSTRALIAN CITIZENS: Australian citizens need only a valid passport to enter Turkey for stays of up to 90 days.

➤ CANADIAN CITIZENS: Canadian citizens need only a valid passport to enter Turkey for stays of up to 90 days.

➤ NEW ZEALAND CITIZENS: New Zealand citizens need only a valid passport to enter Turkey for stays of up to 90 days.

➤ U.K. CITIZENS: Citizens of the U.K. need a valid passport to enter Turkey for stays of up to 90 days and a visa. Visas can be issued at the Turkish embassy or consulate before you go, or at the point of entry; the cost is £10.

➤ U.S. CITIZENS: All U.S. citizens, even infants, need a valid passport and a visa to enter Turkey for stays of up to 90 days. Visas can be issued at the Turkish embassy or consulate before you go, or at the point of entry; the cost is $45 and must be paid in American dollars. If you have plans to go to Greece from Turkey, then return to Turkey, you may have to pay extra or get another visa (even though your visa is supposed to be good for multiple entries).

PASSPORT OFFICES

➤ CONTACT INFORMATION: **Australian Passport Office** (☎ 131–232). **Canadian Passport Office** (☎ 819/994–3500 or 800/567–6868). **New Zealand Passport Office** (☎ 04/494–0700 for information on how to apply, 0800/727–776 for information on applications already submitted). **United Kingdom Passport Office London** (☎ 0990/21010), for fees and documentation requirements

and to request an emergency passport. **United States National Passport Information Center** (☎ 900/225–5674; calls are charged at 35¢ per minute for automated service, $1.05 per minute for operator service).

PUBLIC TRANSPORTATION

BY BOAT

You would expect a sprawling city surrounded by water to be well served by ferries, and Istanbul does not disappoint. The main docks are at Eminönü, on the Old Stamboul side of the Galata Bridge; Karaköy, on the other side of the bridge; Kabataş, near Dolmabahçe Palace; and across the Bosporus on the Asian shore, at Üsküdar and Kadiköy.

Commuter ferries of various sizes crisscross between these points day and night and, like New York's Staten Island Ferry, provide great views of the city at a most reasonable price (usually $3 or less round-trip). One of the most practical and speedy innovations on Istanbul's waterways has been the *deniz otobüsü* (sea buses), which are large, powerful catamarans painted blue, red, and white, operating to and from Karaköy, Kadıköy, Kabataş, Bostancı, the Princes Islands, Yalova, and Bakırköy. The interior is air-conditioned and resembles that of a large aircraft.

The Anadolu Kavağı boat makes all the stops on the European and

Asian sides of the Bosporus. It leaves year-round from the Eminönü Docks, Pier 5, next to the Galata Bridge on the Old Stamboul side, at 10:35 and 1:35, with two extra trips on weekdays and four extra trips on Sunday from April through August. Unless you speak Turkish, have your hotel call for boat schedules, as English is rarely spoken at the docks. The round-trip fare is $6; the ride each way lasts one hour and 45 minutes. You can disembark at any of the stops and pick up a later boat, or return by taxi, dolmuş, or bus.

➤ INFORMATION: Best for sightseeing is the **Anadolu Kavağı** boat (☎ 212/522–0045). Ferry schedules are available at docks marked DENIZ OTOBÜSÜ TERMINALI and are also available on a 24-hour Turkish-language telephone service (☎ 216/362–0444). Information on all city ferries is available between 9 and 5 from the Istanbul **Ferry Lines** office (☎ 212/244–4233).

BY BUS OR TRAM

The city's buses (mostly vermilion and blue, although an increasing number are now completely covered in brightly colored advertising) and trams are crowded and slow, but they are useful for getting around and—at about 50¢ per ride—inexpensive. The route name and number are posted on the front of each vehicle; curbside signboards list routes and itineraries. Buy tickets before

boarding; they're available individually and in books of 10 at stands near the stop or newsstands around the city, and, for a few cents above face value, can also be purchased from shoeshine boys and men sitting on wooden crates at most bus stops. London-style double-deckers operate between Sultanahmet and Emirgan on the Bosporus and between Taksim and Bostancı on the Asian side. Unlike the older city buses, these are clean and offer a panoramic ride. A bus attendant collects fares of three individual tickets (totaling $1.50).

BY TAXI OR DOLMUŞ

Taxis in Istanbul cost about $1 for 1 km (50% higher between midnight and 6 AM). Most drivers do not speak English and may not know every street, so write down the name of the one you want and those nearby and the name of the neighborhood you're visiting. Make sure that the meter says *gunduz* (day rate), otherwise you'll be overcharged. Be aware that taxi drivers in tourist areas often doctor their meters to charge more. Ask at your hotel about how much a ride should cost. Note that **saying the word *direkt* after giving your destination helps prevent you from getting the "grand tour" of town.** Although tipping is not automatic, it is customary to round off the fare to the nearest 25,000 TL. *See* Tipping, *below.*

Dolmuşes (shared taxis), many of which are bright yellow minibuses, run along various routes. You can sometimes hail a dolmuş on the street, and as with taxis, dolmuş stands are marked by signs. The destination is shown on either a roof sign or a card in the front window. Dolmuş stands are placed at regular intervals. Though the savings over a private taxi are significant, you may find the quarters a little too close for comfort, particularly in summer.

SAFETY

Violent crime against strangers is still very rare in Turkey. The streets of Turkey's major cities are considerably safer than their counterparts in the United States or Western Europe. You should nevertheless watch your valuables, as pickpockets, although not as common as in the U.S. or Europe, do operate in the major cities and tourist areas.

WOMEN TRAVELING ALONE

Although Turkey is a generally safe destination for women traveling alone, women who are unaccompanied by men are likely to be approached and sometimes followed in heavily touristed areas like Istanbul. But to give Turkish men the benefit of the doubt, some are genuinely curious about women from other lands and really do want only to "practice their English." Still, be forewarned that a willingness to converse can easily be misconstrued.

As for clothing, Turkey is not the place for clothing that is short, tight, or bare, or for topless bathing. Longer skirts and shirts and blouses with sleeves, however short, are what it takes to look respectable here. Though it may feel odd, covering your head with a scarf will make things easier on you (it's a good idea to have a scarf in your bag at all times). It also helps if you have the manager of the hotel where you are staying call ahead to the manager of your next hotel to announce your arrival. In their eyes, the call makes you a female who is accounted for, and your next host will feel some responsibility to keep you out of harm's way.

As in any other country, the best course is simply to walk on, if approached, and to avoid potentially troublesome situations, such as deserted neighborhoods at night. Note that in Turkey many hotels, restaurants, and other eating spots identify themselves as being for an *aile* (family) clientele, and many restaurants have special sections for women and children. Depending on how comfortable you are being alone, you may or may not like these areas—away from the action—and you may prefer to take your chances in the main room (though some establishments will resist seating you there).

When traveling alone by bus you should request a seat next to another woman.

SHOPPING

Beware of antiques. If you purchase a piece purported to be more than 100 years old, chances are you will end up with an expensive fake, which is just as well since it's illegal to export the real thing without a government permit (and they are very strict about this). If what you covet is less than 100 years old, snap it up. If your purchase looks old, it is advisable to have its date authenticated by a local museum to avoid problems when you leave the country.

Note, too, that Turkish antiquities laws apply to every piece of detritus, so **you shouldn't pick up anything off the ground at archaeological sites.** You may be offered *eski para* (old money) and other "antiquities"; these are all fake and if they were not, they couldn't be taken out of the country. You are much better off buying high quality copies from museum gift shops rather than from peddlers at archaeological sites.

If you buy a rug or kilim and can manage to take it home on the plane, do that. If you have purchased a number of rugs, you might consider shipping them yourself (or letting the store do it for you if it has a good reputation). Note, however, that you are taking a risk by shipping your rug and that it will probably take a while to get to you.

BARGAINING

Outside the bazaars, prices are often fixed, though in tourist areas many shopkeepers will bargain if you ask for a better price. But in bazaars, the operative word is "bargain." More social ritual than battle of wills, it can be great fun once you get the hang of it. As a rule of thumb, offer about 60% of the asking price and be prepared to go up to about 70% to 75%. Note, however, that **it's bad manners and bad business to grossly underbid or to start bargaining if you're not serious about buying.**

SIGHTSEEING TOURS

Arrangements for guided tours can be made through travel agencies (☞ *below*); the offerings are all pretty similar, though names may change. Classical Tours take in Aya Sofya, the Museum of Turkish and Islamic Arts, the Hippodrome, Yerebatan Sarayı, and the Blue Mosque in its half-day versions ($25); the Topkapı Palace, Süleymaniye Cami, the Grand or perhaps the Egyptian Bazaar, and lunch in addition to the above sights in its full-day version ($50; $60–$80 by private car). Bosporus Tours usually include lunch at Sarıyer and visits to the Dolmabahçe and Beylerbeyi palaces. The Night Tour ($50) includes dinner, drinks, and a show at either the Kervansaray or the Galata Tower nightclub.

TELEPHONES

The country code for Turkey is 90. When dialing a Turkish number from abroad, drop the initial 0 from the local area code.

Telephone numbers in Turkey have seven-digit local numbers preceded by a three-digit city code. Intercity lines are reached by dialing 0 before the area code and number. In Istanbul, European and Asian Istanbul have separate area codes: The code for European Istanbul (for numbers beginning with 2, 5, 6, or 8) is 212 (making the number look like it's in New York City—but it's not), and the code for Asian Istanbul (numbers beginning with 3 or 4) is 216.

DIRECTORY & OPERATOR INFORMATION

For international operator services, dial 115. Intercity telephone operators seldom speak English, although international operators usually have some basic English. If you need international dialing codes and assistance, or phone books, you can also go to the nearest post office.

INTERNATIONAL CALLS

To make an international call from a public phone in Turkey, dial 00, then dial the country code, area or city code, and the number. Expect to pay about $3–$5 per minute.

International access codes make calling the United States relatively convenient; check with your long-distance carrier before leaving home. Note that you may find the local access number blocked in many hotel rooms. First ask the hotel operator to connect you. If the hotel operator balks, ask for an international operator, or dial the international operator yourself. One way to improve your odds of getting connected to your long-distance carrier is to travel with more than one company's calling card (a hotel may block Sprint, for example, but not MCI). If all else fails, call from a pay phone in the hotel lobby.

➤ ACCESS CODES: **AT&T Direct** (☎ 00800/12277). **MCI World-Phone** (☎ 00800/11177). **Sprint International Access** (☎ 00800/14477).

LONG-DISTANCE CALLS

To call long-distance within Turkey, dial 131 if you need operator assistance; otherwise dial 0, then dial the city code and number.

PUBLIC PHONES

Most pay phones are blue, push-button models, although a few older, operator-controlled telephones are still in use. Directions in English and other languages are often posted in phone booths.

Public phones either use phone cards (particularly in major cities) or *jetons* (tokens). Available in 7¢ and 30¢ denominations, tokens can be purchased at post offices and street booths. Phone cards can also be purchased at post offices and hotels in denominations of 30 ($2), 60 ($3.50), and 100 ($5) units; buy a 60 or 100 for long-distance calls within Turkey, a 30 for local usage. Cards are sometimes difficult to find, so it's a good idea to buy one at the first opportunity.

To make a local call, insert your phone card or deposit a 7¢ token, wait until the light at the top of the phone goes off, and then dial the number.

TIPPING

In restaurants, a 10% to 15% charge is added to the bill in all but inexpensive, fast-food spots. However, since this money does not necessarily find its way to your waiter, leave an additional 10% on the table. In top establishments, waiters expect tips of 10% to 15% in addition to the service charge. While it's acceptable to include the tip on your bill in restaurants that accept credit cards, a small tip in cash is much appreciated.

Hotel porters expect about $2. Taxi drivers are becoming used to foreigners giving them something; round off the fare to the nearest 25,000 TL. At Turkish baths, the staff that attends you expects to share a tip of 30% to 35% of the bill. Don't worry about missing them—they'll be lined up expectantly on your departure.

Tour guides often expect a tip. Offer as much or (as little) as you feel the person deserves, usually $4–$5 per day if you were happy with the guide. If you've been with the guide for a number of days, tip more. Crews on chartered boats also expect tips.

TRAIN TRAVEL

The term "express train" is a misnomer in Turkey. Although they exist, serving several long-distance routes, they tend to be slow. The overnight sleeper from Istanbul to Ankara (*Ankara Ekspres*) is the most comfortable and convenient of the trains, with private compartments, attentive service, and a candlelit dining car. There is also daytime service between Ankara and Istanbul. In addition, trains run between Istanbul and Edirne.

Fares are lower for trains than for buses (but trains are not as comfortable as buses), and round-trips cost less than two one-way tickets. Student discounts are 10% (30% from December through April). Ticket windows in railroad stations are marked GIŞELERI. Post offices and authorized travel agencies also sell train tickets. It's advisable to **book in advance, in person, for seats on the best trains and for sleeping quarters.**

THE ORIENT EXPRESS

If you have the time—and money—consider the still glamorous Venice Simplon–Orient Express. The route runs twice a year from Paris to Istanbul via Budapest and Bucharest. The return trip runs from Istanbul to Venice. The trip takes five to six days and meals are included.

➤ INFORMATION: **Venice Simplon–Orient Express** (⊠ Sea Containers House, 20 Upper Ground, London SE1 9PF, ☎ 0171/928–6000; 800/524–2420 in the U.S.).

TRAVEL AGENCIES

Most travel agencies are along Cumhuriyet Caddesi, off Taksim Square, in the hotel area: **American Express** (⊠ Istanbul Hilton, Cumhuriyet Cad., Harbiye, ☎ 212/241–0248 or 212/241–0249); **Ekin Tourism** (⊠ Cumhuriyet Cad. 295, Harbiye, ☎ 212/234–4300); **Intra** (⊠ Halâskârgazi Cad. 111–2, Harbiye, ☎ 212/234–1200); **Setur** (⊠ Cumhuriyet Cad. 107, Harbiye, ☎ 212/230–0336); and **Vip Turizm** (⊠ Cumhuriyet Cad. 269/2, Harbiye, ☎ 212/241–6514).

VISITOR INFORMATION

➤ IN ISTANBUL: **Turkish Ministry of Tourism** (⊠ Atatürk Airport, ☎ 212/663–0704; ⊠ Istanbul Hilton, Cumhuriyet Cad., Harbiye, ☎ 212/663–0592; ⊠ International Maritime Passenger Terminal, Karaköy Meyd., ☎ 212/249–5776; in the Sultanahmet district, ⊠ Divan Yolu Cad. 3, ☎ 212/518–1802; and in the Beyoğlu district, ⊠ Meşrutiyet Cad. 57, ☎ 212/245–0109).

Hours are usually from 9 until 5, though some close for an hour around noon.

➤ TURKISH TOURISM OFFICES ABROAD: **Australia** (⊠ 280 George St., Suite 101, Sydney, NSW-2000, ☎ 02/9223–3055). **Canada** (⊠ Constitution Sq., 360 Albert St., Suite 801, Ottawa, Ontario K1R 7X7, ☎ 613/230–8654, ☎ 613/230–3683). **U.K.** (⊠ 170–173 Piccadilly, 1st Floor, London W1V 9DD, ☎ 0171/629–7771). **U.S.** (⊠ 821 UN Plaza, New York, NY 10017, ☎ 212/687–2194, ☎ 212/599–7568; ⊠ 1717 Massachusetts Ave. NW, Suite 306, Washington, DC 20036, ☎ 202/429–9844, ☎ 202/429–5649).

WEB SITES

Do **check out the World Wide Web when you're planning.** You'll find everything from up-to-date weather forecasts to virtual tours of famous cities. Fodor's Web site, www.fodors.com, is a great place to start your on-line travels. For more information specifically on Turkey, visit some of the following.

➤ URLs: **Republic of Turkey** (www.turkey.org). **Travel in Turkey** (www.mersina.com; www.turkiye-online.com; www.exploreturkey.com). **Turkish Airlines** (www.turkishairlines.com).

WHEN TO GO

Most tourists visit between April and the end of October. July and August are the busiest months (and the hottest). April through June, September, and October offer more temperate weather, smaller crowds, and somewhat lower hotel prices. Istanbul tends to be hot in summer, cold in winter.

CLIMATE

The following are the average daily maximum and minimum temperatures for Istanbul.

Climate in Istanbul

Jan.	46F	8C	May	69F	21C	Sept.	76F	24C
	37	3		53	12		61	16
Feb.	47F	9C	June	77F	25C	Oct.	68F	20C
	36	2		60	16		55	13
Mar.	51F	11C	July	82F	28C	Nov.	59F	15C
	38	3		65	18		48	9
Apr.	60F	16C	Aug.	82F	28C	Dec.	51F	11C
	45	7		66	19		41	5

1 Destination: Istanbul

TALES OF THE CITY

THOUGH it is often remarked that Turkey straddles Europe and Asia, it is really Istanbul that does the straddling: The vast bulk of the country resides comfortably on the Asian side. European Istanbul is separated from its Asian suburbs by the Bosporus, the narrow channel that connects the Black Sea, north of the city, to the Sea of Marmara, to the south. (From there it is only a short sail to that superhighway of the ancient world, the Aegean.) The European side of Istanbul is itself divided by a body of water, the Golden Horn, an 8-km-long (5-mi-long) inlet that separates Old Stamboul, also called Old Istanbul, from the "new town," known as Beyoğlu. The Byzantines once stretched an enormous chain across the mouth of the Golden Horn in hopes of protecting their capital city from naval attack. The tactic worked for a time but ultimately failed, after the young Ottoman sultan Mehmet II (ruled 1451–81) had his ships dragged overland from the Bosporus and dropped in behind the chain.

To be sure, more than a mere accident of geography destined Istanbul for greatness. Much of the city's character and fame was created by the sheer force of will of four men. The town of Byzantium was already 1,000 years old when, in AD 326, Emperor Constantine the Great began to enlarge and rebuild it as the new capital of the Roman Empire. On May 11, 330, the city was officially renamed "New Rome," although it soon became better known as Constantinople, the city of Constantine. The new Byzantine empire in the East survived long after the Roman Empire had crumbled in the West.

Under the Byzantine emperor Justinian (ruled 527–565), Constantine's capital flourished. Justinian ordered the construction of the magnificent Hagia Sophia (known as the Aya Sofya in Turkish and referred to throughout this book as such) in 532, on the site of a church originally built for Constantine. This awe-inspiring architectural wonder, which still dominates Istanbul's skyline, spawned untold imitators: Its form is copied by many mosques in the city and elsewhere in Turkey, most notably the Blue Mosque, which sits across Sultanahmet Square like a massive bookend. Under the Byzantines, Constantinople grew to become the largest metropolis the Western world had ever seen. Contemporaries often referred to it simply as the City.

The Ottoman sultan Mehmet II, known as Fatih (the Conqueror), is responsible for the fact that the Hagia Sophia clones are mosques and not churches. It was Mehmet who conquered the long-neglected, nearly ruined Constantinople in 1453, rebuilt it, and made it once again the capital of a great empire. In time it became known as Istanbul (from the Greek *eis tin polin,* meaning "to the city"). In 1468 Mehmet II began building a palace on the picturesque hill at the tip of the city where the Golden Horn meets the Bosporus. Later sultans embellished and extended the building until it grew into the fabulous Topkapı Palace, which can still be seen today.

But most of the finest Ottoman buildings in Istanbul date from the time of Süleyman the Magnificent (ruled 1520–1566), who led the Ottoman Empire to its highest achievements in art and architecture, literature, and law. Süleyman commissioned the brilliant architect Sinan to design buildings that are now recognized as some of the greatest examples of Islamic architecture in the world, including mosques such as the magnificent Süleymaniye, the intimate Sokollu Mehmet Paşa, and the exquisitely tiled Rüstem Paşa.

STANBUL has its modern side, too, with all the concomitant traffic jams, air pollution, overdevelopment, and brash concrete-and-glass hotels creeping up behind its historic old palaces. But the city is more than grime and noise. Paradoxically, its beauty lies in part in the juxtaposition of the ancient and the contemporary. Some of the perks that come with modernity are luxury hotels, designer clothing stores, and Western-style department stores. These are today's monuments, which, alongside the elegant mosques and majestic palaces built by and for yesterday's titans, dominate and define splendid Istanbul.

New and Noteworthy

Turkey's age-old search for identity took a new twist in early 1998 when the **pro-Islamic Welfare Party**, the largest party in parliament, was banned by the Turkish courts under pressure from the country's pro-Western establishment. In June 1997 the Establishment, headed by the fiercely secular military, had worked behind the scenes to bring about the collapse of a one-year-old coalition government headed by the Welfare Party. The party had enjoyed considerable support among Turkey's poor. The domestic political uncertainty that has plagued Turkey throughout the 1990s intensified again in November 1998 when the ruling tripartite coalition government was forced to resign after losing a vote of confidence, leaving the country's politicians to try to stitch together what would be Turkey's seventh government in less than 40 months.

The long-running struggle between Islamists and secularists for the soul of Turkey has left little time to tackle the country's **chronic inflation.** In May 1998 annual inflation in Turkey remained at more than 90 percent, but in dollar terms it was nevertheless still one of the cheapest countries in Europe.

In mid-1998 there was still no sign of a solution to the bloody struggle between the Turkish military and the separatist **Kurdish nationalists,** the PKK, which has claimed more than 27,000 lives since 1983. Despite occasional incidents in Turkey's major cities, the fighting remains mostly concentrated in rural areas in the underdeveloped, and predominantly Kurdish, southeast of the country.

Since the mid-1990s the Turkish military has regained control of most major highways, particularly by day, but security remains high, and there are frequent roadblocks. The PKK has occasionally attacked Western property in the southeast and has been known to seize tourists traveling in the region and hold them hostage in an attempt to gain publicity. Both the State Department of the United States and the British Embassy in Ankara advise their citizens not to visit the area, or if they do go there, to remain within the major cities and either fly or travel by public transport on main roads (the latter during daylight hours only). For an up-to-date report on the situation, call the State Department hot line in Washington, D.C. (☎ 202/647–5225).

Pleasures and Pastimes

Dining

CUISINE

Turkish cuisine is full of vegetables, grains, fresh fish, and seemingly infinite varieties of lamb. Fish and meat are typically served grilled or roasted, although often with inordinate amounts of *yağ* (oil). The core group of seasonings is garlic, sage, oregano, cumin, mint, dill, lemon, and yogurt, always more yogurt. Turkish yogurt is among the tastiest in the world: Many travelers swear it helps keep their stomachs calm and stable while on the road.

This guide makes frequent references to "traditional Turkish cuisine." Here's what to expect.

MEZES➤ Select from a variety of these appetizers brought to your table with a basket of bread. Standard cold mezes include *patlıcan salatası* (roasted eggplant puree flavored with garlic and lemon), *haydarı* (a thick yogurt dip made with garlic and dill), *dolma* (stuffed grape leaves, peppers, or mussels), *ezme* (a spicy paste of tomatoes, minced green pepper, onion, and parsley), *kızartma* (deep-fried eggplant, zucchini, or green pepper served with fresh yogurt), *cacık* (a garlicky cold yogurt "soup" with shredded cucumber, mint, or dill), *barbunya pilaki* (kidney beans, tomatoes, and onions cooked in olive oil), and *barbunya pilaki* (slow-roasted baby eggplant topped with olive oil–fried onions and tomatoes and seasoned with garlic). One taste of this last meze, and you'll understand how it got its name—which means, "The imam fainted with delight." Inevitably there will be other dishes based on eggplant, *patlıcan* in Turkish. Hot appetizers, usually called *ara sıcak,* include *börek* (a deep-fried or oven-baked pastry filled with cheese or meat), *kalamar* (deep-fried calamari served with a special sauce), and *midye tava* (deep-fried mussels).

KEBABS➤ Available almost any place you stop to eat, kebabs (*kebaps* in Turkish) come in many guises. Although the ingredient of choice for Turks is lamb, some kebabs are made with beef, chicken, or fish, usually grilled with vegetables on a skewer. *Adana kebaps* are spicy ground-lamb patties arranged on a layer of sautéed pita bread, topped with a zippy yogurt-and-garlic sauce. *İskender kebaps,* also known as *Bursa kebaps,* are sliced grilled lamb, smothered in tomato sauce, hot butter, and yogurt. *Şiş kebaps* are the traditional skewered cubes of lamb, usually interspersed with peppers and onions. *Köfte kebaps* are meatballs made from minced lamb mixed with rice, bulgur, or bread crumbs, then threaded onto skewers.

FISH AND MEAT➤ Fresh fish, often a main course, is commonly served grilled and drizzled with olive oil and lemon. You will find *alabalık* (trout), *barbunya* (red mullet), *kalkan* (turbot), *kefal* (gray mullet), *kılıç* (swordfish, sometimes served as a kebab), *levrek* (sea bass), *lüfer* (bluefish), and *palamut* (bonito). In the meat department, there is *mantı,* a sort of Turkish ravioli served with garlicky yogurt that has a touch of mint. Grilled quail is most common inland; it's often marinated in tomatoes, yogurt, olive oil, and cinnamon. *Karışık ızgara,* a mixed grill, usually combines tender chicken breast, beef, a lamb chop, and spicy lamb patties, all served with rice pilaf and vegetables. *Tandır kebap,* lamb cooked in a pit, is a typical Anatolian dish.

DESSERTS➤ You'll encounter several varieties of *baklava* (phyllo pastry with honey and chopped nuts) and *burma kadayıf* (shredded wheat in honey or syrup). Also popular are puddings, made of yogurt and eggs, and sweet rice or milk and rice flour.

BREAKFAST➤ Usually eaten at your hotel, breakfast typically consists of *beyaz peynir* (goat cheese), sliced tomatoes, cucumbers, and olives, with a side order of fresh bread; the menu varies little, whether you stay in a simple pansiyon or an upscale hotel. Yogurt with honey and fresh fruit is generally available as well, as are tea and coffee.

TYPES OF RESTAURANTS

The simplest establishments, Turkey's fast-food joints, are the *kebapçı*, the *dönerçı*, and the *pideçı*. The first specializes in kebabs—marinated cubes of meat (generally lamb), usually grilled and cooked with vegetables on a skewer. Dönerçıs provide a quick meal of spicy, spit-roasted sliced lamb, served either as a sandwich or with rice. At the pideçı, you'll find *pide,* a pizzalike snack made of flat bread topped with either butter, cheese, and egg or ground lamb and baked in a wood-fired oven. Often these eateries are little more than counters at which you belly up to the bar for instant gratification; on occasion they attain luncheonette status.

Lokantas are unpretentious neighborhood spots that make up the vast majority of Turkish restaurants. Lokantas are frequently open-air, the better to take advantage of the waterfront and sky, or are surrounded by flower-filled trellises. Often you serve yourself cafeteria style from big display cases full of hot and cold dishes—a relief if you don't speak Turkish. If there is no menu, it is because the chef only serves what is fresh, and that changes from day to day.

In the more upscale *restorans* (restaurants), you can expect tablecloths, menus, even a wine list, and dishes drawn from the richer, "palace" cuisine of Turkish royalty, often with Continental touches.

WINE, BEER, AND SPIRITS

Alcohol is readily available and widely consumed, despite Turkey's predominantly Muslim culture. Among the perfectly acceptable, inexpensive local wines, the best are Villa Doluca and Kavaklidere, available in *beyaz* (white) and *kırmızı* (red). The most popular local beer is Efes Pilsen, your basic American-type pilsner. In late 1997 Efes also started making a black beer called Efes Dark, and Tuborg pilsner is brewed under license in Turkey. In upscale bars and hotels it is also sometimes possible to find imported beers such as Budweiser. The national drink is *rakı,* a relative of the Greek ouzo, made from grapes and aniseed. Usually it's mixed with water or ice, though many connoisseurs insist that it's best drunk neat, with each sip of rakı followed immediately by a sip of cold water. People drink it throughout their meal or as an aperitif.

Marketplaces

Atatürk moved the political capital to Ankara, but Turkey's commercial heart still beats in

Istanbul. The city is a hive of free enterprise. Wherever you look, something is being traded: stocks or shares on Turkey's stock exchange; rugs; leather and jewelry in the 4,000 shops of the ancient Grand Bazaar; spices and dried fruit in the Egyptian Bazaar; fruit, vegetables, and clothing in the city's numerous open markets; and flowers, toolkits, soft drinks, and the many wares that children hawk as they weave through rush-hour traffic.

Museums

Until the early 1980s Istanbul, with its crumbling ancient buildings, was its own best museum. Most artifacts of the city's past were locked away in storage areas or poorly displayed in dusty, badly lit rooms. But in recent years Istanbul's museums have been transformed. Topkapı Palace, which for 400 years was the palace of the Ottoman sultans, contains a glittering array of jewels, ceramics, miniature paintings, and holy relics. The Archaeological Museum houses one of the most important collections of classical artifacts anywhere in the world. The Museum of Turkish and Islamic Arts holds superb examples of artistry and craftsmanship.

Outdoor Activities and Sports

BEACHES ➤ Even though local boys playfully dive into the sea even in the heart of the city, swimming is not recommended. The European shore of the Sea of Marmara is muddy and unpleasant, the Bosporus is famous for its dangerously strong currents, and either way, the water is pretty cold and heavily polluted. Stick with the hotel pool.

GOLF ➤ Istanbul is not a noted golfing destination; you won't find Sawgrass or Pebble Beach, but the courses are perfectly fine if you need a fix. Itinerant players are welcomed at the **Golf Club** (✉ Büyükdere Cad., Ayazağa, ☎ 212/264–0742). The **Kemer Golf & Country Club** (✉ Kemerburgaz in the Belgrade Forest, 25 mins from Istanbul, ☎ 212/239–7913) has a nine-hole course.

JOGGING AND WALKING ➤ If exploring the city's streets still leaves you wanting more exercise, try one of its parks. The wooded slopes of **Yıldız Park,** just north of the Çırağan Palace, are usually blissfully uncrowded. **Belgrade Forest** has enticing wooded paths and a 6.5-km (4-mi) walking and jogging track around the shores of old reservoirs. **Emirgân Park** is noted for its flower gardens and Bosporus views. **Gülhane Park** is conveniently located, right alongside Topkapı Palace.

SOCCER ➤ Soccer is Turkey's passion, and **Turkish Division One** is the country's major league. Matches take place from September through May at İnönü Stadium, Fenerbahçe Stadium, and Ali Sami Yen Stadium. You can get tickets at the stadiums or ask at your hotel for help. If you prefer comfort to atmosphere, ask someone at your hotel—almost everyone is a passionate fan of one of the city's teams—for the schedule of televised games.

Shopping

The bazaars, all brimming with copper and brassware, hand-painted ceramics, carved alabaster and onyx, fabrics, richly colored carpets, and (truth be told) tons of tourist junk, are the main places to shop in Turkey. You won't roam the bazaars too long before someone tries to lure you in with a free glass of *çay* (tea), whether you're a serious shopper or are just browsing. Remember that bargaining is essential.

For more about shopping in Istanbul, *see* Essential Information and Chapter 6.

RUGS

Persistent salesmen and affordable prices make it hard to leave Turkey without flat-woven kilims or other rugs. No matter what you've planned, sooner or later you'll end up in the cool of a carpet shop listening to a sales rap. Regardless of how many cups of tea you drink and how persistent the salesmen may be, do not let yourself be pressured into making a purchase you do not want. Salesmen will insist they can't lower the price, but they almost always do.

OTHER LOCAL SPECIALTIES

Made of a light, porous stone found only in Turkey, meerschaum pipes are prized for their cool smoke; look for a centered hole and even walls. You can also buy tiles and porcelain, though modern work doesn't compare with older craftsmanship. Some spices, saffron foremost among them, can be purchased for a fraction of their cost back home. Another good deal is jewelry, because you pay by weight and not for design—but watch out for tin and alloys masquerading as silver. Turkey is also known for its leather goods, but it's better to stick with merchandise off the rack and steer clear of made-to-order goods.

Quick Tours

If you're here for just a short period you need to plan carefully so as to make the most of your time in Istanbul. The following itineraries outline major sights throughout the city, and will help you structure your visit efficiently. Each is intended to take about four hours—a perfect way to fill a free morning or afternoon. How much time you spend at each place will depend on your tastes and priorities, but these brief outlines will give you an idea of which sights and areas make for a logical tour of the city. For more information about individual sights, *see* Chapter 2 and Chapter 7.

Topkapı Sarayı

Make your first stop **Topkapı Sarayı,** the vast palace that was at the heart of the Ottoman Empire for more than 400 years and is Istanbul's number-one tourist attraction. You could easily spend two days here, but at least see **the Treasure Room, the Harem,** and **the Porcelain Collection.**

The Blue Mosque and Aya Sofya

After lunch at one of the restaurants lining Divan Yolu in Alemdar, visit the **Blue Mosque**—so named because it's decorated with 20,000 shimmering blue İznik tiles. Afterwards, head across the street to **Aya Sofya,** the world's largest church until St. Peter's Basilica was built, and **Yerebatan Sarnıcı.**

The Egyptian Bazaar and Süleymaniye Cami

The **Egyptian Bazaar,** also known as the Spice Market, is a worthwhile stop on any tour of this commercially vibrant city. Combine a stroll through this marketplace with a visit to the enormous **Süleymaniye Cami.**

The Bosporus

If you can spare a full day, spend it taking a cruise up **the Bosporus.** Even if you only have a few hours, however, a cursory tour via commuter ferry is worthwhile for the incredible views of the city from the water.

2 Exploring Istanbul

HOW DO YOU FIND YOUR BEARINGS in such an unpredictable place? Head for the Galata Bridge, which spans the mouth of the Haliç (Golden Horn). Look to the north, and you will see the new town, modern Beyoğlu, and Taksim Square. From the square, high-rise hotels and smart shops radiate out on all sides. Beyond Taksim lie the fashionable modern shopping districts of Şişli and Nişantaşı. The residential suburbs of Arnavutköy, Bebek, Yeniköy, Tarabya, and Sarıyer line the European shore of the Bosporus. Look southeast, across the Bosporus, and you can see the Asian suburbs of Kadıköy and Üsküdar. To the south lies the old walled city of Stamboul and Sultanahmet (after the sultan who built the Blue Mosque), with Aya Sofya and Topkapı Palace at its heart. Turn to look up the Golden Horn, and you should be able to make out two more bridges, the Atatürk, favored by cab drivers hoping to avoid the Galata Bridge, and the Fatih, out at the city's northwestern edge.

Numbers in the text correspond to numbers in the margin and on the Exploring Istanbul, Topkapı Sarayı, and Bosporus maps.

Old Stamboul

Old Stamboul isn't large, but it can be overwhelming, for it spans vast epochs of history and contains an incredible concentration of art and architecture. The best way to get around is on foot.

A Good Walk

Begin from **Topkapı Sarayı** ①. Walk back past Aya Irini, a smaller-scale version of Aya Sofya. The **Arkeoloji Müzesi** ② is just north of Aya Irini. A small square surrounding a fountain built by Sultan Ahmet III lies just outside the Topkapı Palace gate. Take a right down Soğukçeşme Sokak, a beautiful cobbled street lined with restored wooden Ottoman houses. At the bottom of Soğukçeşme Sokak, just before the entrance to Gülhane Park, take a left up Alemdar Caddesi to **Aya Sofya** ③ and **Yerebatan Sarnıcı** ④. Cross to the far left-hand corner of the small park between Aya Sofya and the **Blue Mosque** ⑤ to Kabasakal Caddesi. Approximately

325 ft along Kabasakal Caddesi is the **Mozaik Müzesi** ⑥, which is believed once to have been the imperial palace of the Byzantine emperors. Backtracking around the southern face of the Blue Mosque, you can see the foundation of the **Hippodrome** ⑦, a Byzantine stadium, stretching northeast for three blocks to Divan Yolu. West of the Hippodrome is **Ibrahim Paşa Sarayı** ⑧; walk to the southwest down Mehmet Paşa Yokuşu to get to **Sokollu Mehmet Paşa Cami** ⑨.

TIMING

Allow approximately 45 minutes to an hour to walk this route, two or more days to take in all its sights. Topkapı Sarayı and the Arkeoloji Müzesi are open daily. The Blue Mosque is also open daily, but the Carpet and Kilim museums within it are closed weekends. Aya Sofya and Ibrahim Paşa Palace are closed Monday, the Mosaic Museum on Tuesday, and the Kariye Museum on Wednesday. It's best not to visit mosques during midday prayers on Friday.

Sights to See

★ ☙ ❷ **Arkeoloji Müzesi** (Archaeology Museum). A fine collection of Greek and Roman antiquities—including pieces from Ephesus and Troy, along with a magnificent tomb believed by some to have belonged to Alexander the Great—is among the museum's highlights. Since most of the pieces have been removed from the archaeological sites of Turkey's ancient cities, touring the museum can help you later to visualize what belongs in the empty niches. Among the museum's sections is one for children, complete with a replica of the Trojan Horse; a special exhibit on Istanbul through the ages; and one on the different settlements at Troy. Because the children's wing is primarily intended for Turkish schoolchildren, the captions there are in Turkish, but the other two have labels in English. Outside the museum is a small garden planted with bits of statuary and tombstones. In summer a small café is open.

Admission to the Arkeoloji Müzesi is also good for entry to the nearby **Eski Şark Eserleri Müzesi** (Museum of the Ancient Orient) and **Çinili Köşkü** (Tiled Pavilion). The first museum is something of a disappointment despite its Sumerian, Babylonian, and Hittite treasures. The place needs a fresh coat of paint, the displays are unimaginative, and the descriptions of what you see are terse at best. The Tiled Pavilion has ceramics from the early Seljuk and Ottoman empires and tiles from İznik, which produced perhaps the finest ceramics in the world during the 17th and 18th centuries. Covered in a bright profusion of colored tiles, the building itself is part of the exhibit. ⊠ *Gülhane Park, adjacent to Topkapı Palace,* ☎ *212/520–7740.* ⬜ *$2 (total) for the 3 museums.* ⊙ *Archaeology Museum: Tues.–Sun. 9:30–4:30; Tiled Pavilion: Tues.–Sun. 9:30–noon; Museum of the Ancient Orient: Tues.–Sun. 1–5.*

★ ❸ **Aya Sofya** (Hagia Sophia). The magnificent dome of Aya Sofya, more commonly known as Hagia Sophia (Church of the Holy Wisdom), was the world's largest church until St. Peter's Basilica was built in Rome 1,000 years later. It was considered miraculous by the faithful. Though some were afraid to enter lest the whole thing come crashing down, others argued that the fact that it didn't was proof that God was on their side. Nothing like the dome's construction had ever been attempted before—new architectural rules had to be made up as the builders went along. Perhaps the greatest work of Byzantine architecture, the cathedral was Christendom's most important church for 900 years. It survived earthquakes, looting crusaders, and the city's conquest by Mehmet the Conqueror in 1453. The church was then converted into a mosque; its four minarets were added by succeeding sultans.

The Byzantine mosaics were not destroyed but were plastered over in the 16th century at the behest of Süleyman the Magnificent in accordance with the Islamic proscription against the portrayal of the human figure in a place of worship. In 1936 Atatürk made Aya Sofya into a museum. Shortly thereafter American archaeologists rediscovered the mosaics, which were restored and are now on display. Above where the altar would have been is a giant portrait of a somber Virgin Mary with the infant Jesus, and alongside are severe-looking depictions of archangels Michael and Gabriel.

Ascend to the gallery above, and you will find the best of the remaining mosaics, executed in the 13th century. There is a group with Emperor John Comnenus, the Empress Zoë and her husband (actually, her third husband; his face was added atop his predecessors'), and Jesus with Mary, and

14

Exploring Istanbul

KEY

AE American Express Office

i Tourist Information

0 ___ 440 yards

0 ___ 400 meters

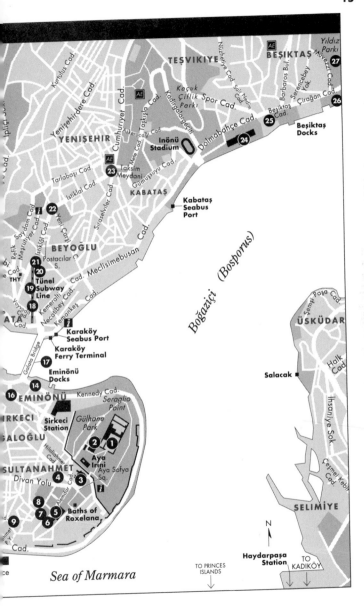

TEŞVIKIYE

BEŞIKTAŞ

Yıldız Parkı

27

Müvezzi Cad.

Nüzhetiye Cad.

Barbaros Bul.

Kuruluş Cad.

Kemalus Cad.

Yenişehirdere Cad.

Köçük Çiftlik Spor Cad. Parkı

Kadırgalarağrı

Serençebey Yok.

Çırağan Cad.

26

25

Beşiktaş Cad.

YENIŞEHIR

Cumhuriyet Cad.

İnönü Stadium

Dolmabahçe Cad.

Beşiktaş Docks

24

Askerocağı Cad.

Mete Cad. Taşkışla Cad.

23

Tarlabaşı Cad.

Taksim Meydanı

Gümüşsuyu Cad.

KABATAŞ

İstiklâl Cad.

Sıraselviler Cad.

Kabataş Seabus Port

22

Yeni Çarşı

Saydam Cad.

Meşrutiyet Cad.

Meclisimebusan

Cad.

BEYOĞLU

21

Postacılar

İstiklâl Cad.

S.

Boğaziçi (Bosporus)

THY

20

Kemeraltı Cad.

19 Tünel Subway Line

ÜSKÜDAR

Necatibey Cad.

Kemankeş

Şemsi Paşa Cad.

18

Vorvoda Cad.

ATA Cad.

Karaköy Seabus Port

Karaköy Ferry Terminal

Halk Cad.

17

Galata Bridge

Eminönü Docks

14

16 EMINÖNÜ

Kennedy Cad.

Seraglio Point

İhsaniye Sok.

Salacak ■

IRKECI Sirkeci Station

Gülhane Park

GALOĞLU

1

2

Çeşmei Kebir Cad.

SULTANAHMET

Hilaliahmer Cad.

Aya İrini

Aya Sofya Sq.

Divan Yolu

4

3

Alemdar Cad.

8

5

Baths of Roxelana

SELIMIYE

7

6

9

N

Sea of Marmara

Haydarpaşa Station

TO KADIKÖY

TO PRINCES ISLANDS

ce

another of John the Baptist. According to legend, the marble-and-brass **Sacred Column** in the north aisle of the mosque weeps water that can work miracles. It's so popular that over the centuries believers have worn a hole through the column with their constant caresses. Today visitors of many faiths stick their fingers in the hole and make a wish; nobody will mind if you do so as well. In recent years there has been growing pressure for Aya Sofya to be reopened for Muslim worship. Some radical elements often gather to pray at the museum at midday on Friday. As with mosques, it is best not to try to visit then. ⊠ *Aya Sofya Sq.,* ☎ *212/522–1750.* ▣ *$4.50.* ☉ *Tues.– Sun. 9:30–4:30.*

NEED A BREAK?

For a real treat, spend an hour in a Turkish bath. One of the best is **Cağaloğlu Hamamı** (⊠ Prof. Kazı Gürkan Cad. 34, Cağaloğlu, ☎ 212/522-2424), in a magnificent 18th-century building near Aya Sofya. Florence Nightingale and Kaiser Wilhelm II once soaked here; the clientele today remains generally upscale (Turks of lesser means head for plainer, less costly baths). You get a cubicle in which to strip down—and a towel to cover yourself with—and are then escorted into a steamy, marble-clad temple to cleanliness. Self-service baths cost just $10; an extra $5–$10 buys you that time-honored, punishing-yet-relaxing pummeling known as Turkish massage. The baths are open daily 8–8 for women and until 10 PM for men.

★ ❺ **Blue Mosque** (Sultan Ahmet Cami). This massive structure, officially called Sultan Ahmet Cami (Mosque of Sultan Ahmet), is studded with mini- and semidomes and surrounded by six minarets. This number briefly linked it with the Elharam Mosque in Mecca, until Sultan Ahmet I (ruled 1603–17) was forced to send his architect down to the Holy City to build a seventh minaret and reestablish Elharam's eminence. Press through the throng of people trying to sell you things, and enter the mosque at the side entrance that faces Aya Sofya. You must remove your shoes and leave them at the entrance. Immodest clothing is not allowed, but an attendant at the door will lend you a robe if he feels you are not dressed appropriately. Women should cover their heads.

Only after you enter the Blue Mosque do you understand why it is so named. Inside it's decorated with 20,000 shimmering blue İznik tiles interspersed with 260 stained-glass windows; an airy arabesque pattern is painted on the ceiling. After the dark corners and stern, sour faces of the Byzantine mosaics in Aya Sofya, this light-filled mosque is positively cheery. Architect Mehmet Aga, known as Sedefkar (Worker of Mother-of-Pearl), spent eight years getting the mosque just right, beginning in 1609. His goal, set by Sultan Ahmet, was to surpass Justinian's masterpiece—completed nearly 1,100 years earlier—and many believe he succeeded.

The **Hünkar Kasrı** (Carpet and Kilim museums), two good places to prepare yourself for dueling with modern-day carpet dealers, are in the stone-vaulted cellars of the Blue Mosque and upstairs at the end of a stone ramp, where the sultans rested before and after their prayers. Here rugs are treated as works of art and displayed in a suitably grand setting. ⊠ *Sultanahmet Sq.,* ☎ *212/518–1330 for museum information only.* ▨ *Mosque free; museums $1.50.* ☉ *Blue Mosque: daily 9–5, access restricted during prayer times, particularly at midday on Fri.; museums: weekdays 8:30–noon and 1–3:30.*

❼ **Hippodrome.** Once a Byzantine stadium with 100,000 seats, the Hippodrome was the center for public entertainment, including chariot races and circuses. Disputes between rival groups of supporters of chariot teams often degenerated into violence. Thirty thousand people died here in what came to be known as the Nike riots of AD 531. The original shape of the Hippodrome is still clearly visible. The monuments that can be seen today on the grassy open space opposite the Blue Mosque—the **Egyptian Obelisk** (Dikilitaş) from the 15th century BC, the **Column of Constantinos** (Örme Sütün), and the **Serpentine Column** (Yılanlı Sütun), taken from the Temple of Apollo at Delphi in Greece—formed part of the central barrier around which the chariots raced. The Hippodrome was originally adorned with a life-size sculpture of four horses cast in bronze. That piece was taken by the Venetians and can now be seen at the entrance to the Cathedral of San Marco in Venice. In this area you'll encounter hundreds of peddlers selling postcards, nuts, and souvenirs. ⊠ *Atmeydanı, Sultanahmet.* ▨ *Free.* ☉ *Accessible at all hrs.*

★ **8** **Ibrahim Paşa Sarayı** (Ibrahim Paşa Palace). The grandiose residence of the son-in-law and grand vizier of Süleyman the Magnificent was built circa 1524. The striated stone mansion was outfitted by Süleyman to be the finest private residence in Istanbul, but Ibrahim Paşa didn't have long to enjoy it: He was executed when he became too powerful for the liking of Süleyman's power-crazed wife, Roxelana. The palace now houses the **Türk Ve Islâm Eserleri Müzesi** (Museum of Turkish and Islamic Arts), where you can get insight into the lifestyles of Turks at every level of society, from the 8th century to the present. ⊠ *Atmeydanı 46, Sultanahmet,* ☏ *212/518–1385.* ☞ *$2.* ☉ *Tues.–Sun. 9–4.*

6 **Mozaik Müzesi** (Mosaic Museum). Tucked away behind the Blue Mosque, the often-overlooked Mosaic Museum is actually the ruins of the Great Palace of Byzantium, the imperial residence of the Byzantine emperors when they ruled lands stretching from Iran to Italy. The mosaics that give the museum its name lay hidden underground for 1,000 years before being uncovered by archaeologists in 1935. Scenes of animals, flowers, and trees in many of the mosaics depict rural idylls far removed from the pomp and elaborate ritual of the imperial court. ⊠ *Kabasakal Cad., Sultanahmet,* ☏ *212/518–1205.* ☞ *$1.50.* ☉ *Wed.–Mon. 9–4.*

9 **Sokollu Mehmet Paşa Cami** (Mosque of Mehmet Paşa). This small mosque, built in 1571, is generally regarded as one of the most beautifully realized projects of the master architect Sinan, who designed more than 350 other buildings and monuments under the direction of Süleyman the Magnificent. Rather than dazzle with size, the mosque integrates all its parts into a harmonious whole, from the courtyard and porticoes outside to the delicately carved *mimber* (pulpit) and well-preserved İznik tiles set off by pure white walls and stained-glass windows done in a floral motif inside. ⊠ *Mehmet Paşa Cad. at Özbekler Sok., Küçük Ayasofya,* ☏ *no phone.* ☞ *Free.* ☉ *Daily sunrise–sunset, except during prayer times.*

★ **1** **Topkapı Sarayı** (Topkapı Palace). Istanbul's number-one attraction sits on Seraglio Point, where the Bosporus meets the Golden Horn. The vast palace was the residence of sultans and their harems until 1868, when Sultan Abdül Mecit I (ruled 1839–61) moved to the European-style Dolmabahçe Palace farther up the Bosporus. Plan on spending several hours and go early before the bus-tour crowds pour in; gates open at 9. If you go by taxi, be sure to tell the driver you want the Topkapı Sarayı in Sultanahmet, or you could end up at the Topkapı bus terminal on the outskirts of town.

Sultan Mehmet II built the first palace during the 1450s, shortly after his conquest of Constantinople. Over the centuries sultan after sultan added ever more elaborate architectural frills and fantasies, until the palace had acquired four courtyards and quarters for some 5,000 full-time residents, including slaves, concubines, and eunuchs. The initial approach to the palace does little to evoke the many tales of intrigue, bloodshed, and drama attached to the structure. The first entrance, or Imperial Gate, leads to the **Court of the Janissaries,** also known as the First Courtyard, an area the size of a football field that now serves as a parking lot. As you walk ahead to the ticket office, look to your left, where you will see the **Aya Irini** (Church of St. Irene, Hagia Eirene in Greek). This unadorned redbrick building, now used for concerts, dates to the earliest days of Byzantium.

Formed in the 14th century as the sultan's corps of elite guards, the Janissaries were taken as young boys from non-Muslim families in Ottoman-controlled territories in the Balkans, taught Turkish, and instructed in Islam. Though theoretically the sultan's vassals, these professional soldiers quickly became a power in their own right, and more than once their protests—traditionally expressed by overturning their soup kettles—were followed by the murder of the reigning sultan. During the rule of Sultan Mahmut II (ruled 1808–39), the tables were finally turned, and the Janissaries were massacred in what came to be known as the Auspicious Event.

Next to the ticket office is the **Bab-ı-Selam** (Gate of Salutation), built in 1524 by Süleyman the Magnificent, who was the only person allowed to pass through it on horseback; others had to dismount and enter on foot. Prisoners were kept in the towers on either side before their execution next to the nearby fountain. Once you pass this gate, you begin to get an idea of the grandeur of the palace.

The **Second Courtyard,** just slightly smaller than the first, is planted with rose gardens and ornamental trees and

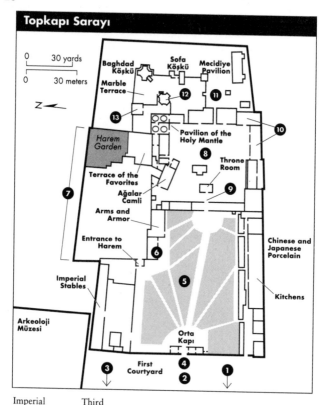

Topkapı Sarayı

0 — 30 yards
0 — 30 meters

Baghdad Köşkü
Sofa Köşkü
Mecidiye Pavilion
Marble Terrace

12
11

13

Harem Garden

Pavilion of the Holy Mantle

10

8

Throne Room

Terrace of the Favorites

Ağalar Camli

9

Arms and Armor

Entrance to Harem

6

Chinese and Japanese Porcelain

5

Kitchens

Imperial Stables

Arkeoloji Müzesi

Orta Kapı

3

First Courtyard

4
2
1

Imperial Gate, **1**
Court of the Janissaries, **2**
Aya Irini, **3**
Bab-ı-Selam, **4**
Second Courtyard, **5**
Divan-ı-Humayun, **6**
Harem, **7**
Third Courtyard, **8**
Bab-ı-Saadet, **9**
Treasury, **10**
Fourth Courtyard, **11**
Rivan Köşkü, **12**
Sünnet Odası, **13**

filled with a series of ornate *köşks,* pavilions once used for both the business of state and for more mundane matters, like feeding the hordes of servants. To the right are the palace's immense kitchens, which now display one of the world's best collections of Chinese porcelain, including 10th-century T'ang, Yuan celadon, and Ming blue-and-white pieces dating from the 18th century, when the Chinese produced pieces to order for the palace. Straight ahead is the **Divan-ı-Humayun** (Assembly Room of the Council of State), once presided over by the grand vizier. When the mood struck him, the sultan would sit behind a latticed window, hidden by a curtain, so no one would know when he was listening, although occasionally he would pull the curtain aside to comment.

One of the most popular sections of Topkapı is the **Harem,** a maze of 400 halls, terraces, rooms, wings, and apartments grouped around the sultan's private quarters to the west of the Second Courtyard. Only 40 rooms, all meticulously restored, are open to the public (and only on tours, which leave every half hour and cost $1.50). But they give you an idea of both the opulence and the regimentation of harem life. Only a few qualified for presentation to the sultan; even then, not all walked the Golden Way, by which the favorite of the night entered the sultan's private quarters. The first areas you see, which housed the palace eunuchs and about 200 lesser concubines, resemble a monastery; the tiny cubicles are as cramped and uncomfortable as the Harem's main rooms are large and opulent. Private apartments around a shared courtyard housed the chief wives (Islamic law permitted up to four); the *valide* sultan (queen mother), the absolute ruler of the Harem, had quite a bit of space as well as her own courtyard and marble bath. The sultan's private rooms are a riot of brocades, murals, colored marble, wildly ornate furniture, gold leaf, and fine carving. Fountains, also much in evidence, were not only decorative—they made it hard to eavesdrop on royal conversations. All told, it is a memorable, worthy backdrop to the rise and fall of princes and pretenders.

You exit the Harem into the somewhat smaller **Third Courtyard.** To see it to best advantage, make your way to its main gate, the **Bab-ı-Saadet** (Gate of Felicity), then exit and reenter. Shaded by regal old trees, the Third Courtyard is dotted by some of the most ornate of the palace's pavilions. Foreign ambassadors once groveled just past the gate in the **Arz Odası** (Audience Chamber), but access to the courtyard was highly restricted, in part because it housed the **Treasury,** four rooms filled with jewels, including two uncut emeralds, each weighing about 8 pounds, that once hung from the ceiling. Here, too, is the dazzling emerald dagger used in the movie *Topkapi* and the 84-carat Spoonmaker diamond, which, according to legend, was found by a pauper and traded for three wooden spoons. Not surprisingly, this is one of the most popular sections of the palace, and it can get quite crowded. Also within this courtyard you can view a collection of thousands of Turkish and Persian miniatures, relics of the prophet Muhammad, and the rich costumes of the Imperial Wardrobe. Imperial fashion (male, of course) evolves slowly in the magnificent display of sultans' robes from the first to the last ruler. Some robes are bloodstained and torn from assassins' daggers; garments are stiff with gold and silver thread, tooled leather, and gold, silver, and jewels.

The **Fourth Courtyard,** the last, contains small, elegant summer houses, mosques, fountains, and reflecting pools scattered amid the gardens. Here you will find the cruciform **Rivan Köşkü,** built by Murat IV in 1636 to commemorate a military victory. In another pavilion, the **İftariye** (Golden Cage), the closest relatives of the reigning sultan, lived in strict confinement under what amounted to house arrest, ostensibly to help keep the peace, although it meant that heirs had no opportunity to prepare themselves for the formidable task of ruling a great empire. The custom began during the 1800s, superseding an older practice of murdering all possible rivals to the throne. Just off the open terrace with the wishing well is the lavishly tiled **Sünnet Odası** (Circumcision Room), where little princes would be taken for ritual circumcision during their 9th or 10th year. ⊠ *Topkapı Palace, Gülhane Park, near Sultanahmet Sq.,* ☎ *212/512–0480.* 🗺 *$3.50, plus $1.50 for harem tour.* ☉ *Wed.–Mon. 9:30–4:30.*

....

NEED A   Just past the Topkapı Palace's Treasury, on the right side of
BREAK?   the courtyard, are steps leading to the 19th-century rococo-
               style Mecidiye Pavilion, also known as the Köşk of Sultan

Abdül Mecit I, for whom it was built. It now houses the **Konyalı Restaurant** (☎ 212/513–9696), which serves traditional Turkish dishes (albeit with a mass-produced flavor) and has magnificent views. On a terrace below is an outdoor café with an even better view. Go early to beat the tour-group crush. The restaurant and the café are open for lunch only.

★ ❹ **Yerebatan Sarnıcı** (Sunken Cistern). Also known as the Basilica Cistern, Yerebatan Sarnıcı is the most impressive part of an underground network of waterways said to have been created at the behest of Emperor Constantine in the 4th century and expanded by Justinian in the 6th century (most of the present structure dates from the Justinian era). The cistern was always kept full as a precaution against long sieges. Today it is an atmospheric space, with 336 marble columns rising 26 ft to support Byzantine arches and domes. Piped-in classical music accompanies the sound of endlessly dripping water. ⊠ *Yerebatan Cad. at Divan Yolu*, ☎ *212/522–1259.* 🎫 *$1.* ☉ *Daily 9–4:30.*

OFF THE BEATEN PATH

KARIYE MÜZESI – Often passed over because of its inconvenient location at Istanbul's western edge, near the remnants of the city's Byzantine walls, the Kariye Museum occupies what was once the Church of the Holy Savior in Chora, erected in the 5th century under the aegis of Justinian and rebuilt several times since. You come to see not the architecture but the dazzling 14th-century mosaics and frescoes depicting biblical scenes from Adam to the life of Christ; they are considered among the finest Byzantine works in the world. The historic Ottoman buildings around the museum have been restored as well. A tea shop on the garden terrace serves light fare. Just west of the Chora are the Constantinian Walls, built by Emperor Theodosius II in AD 413. The massive walls, several stories high and from 10 ft to 20 ft thick in spots, protected Constantinople from onslaught after onslaught by Huns, Bulgarians, Russians, Arabs, Goths, and Turks. The walls were breached only twice: by the crusaders in the 1200s and by Mehmet the Conqueror in 1453. ⊠ *1 block north of Fevzipaşa Cad., by Edirne Gate in city's outer walls*, ☎ *212/631–9241.* 🎫 *$1.50.* ☉ *Thurs.–Tues. 9:30–4.*

Grand Bazaar to Eminönü

This walk leads you through several markets, including two of Istanbul's largest, and takes you to two of the city's most beautiful mosques.

A Good Walk

After a visit to the **Grand Bazaar** ⑩, exit through the front entrance on Yeniçeriler Caddesi and head west to that street's junction with Çadırcı Camii Caddesi. You'll see **Beyazıt Cami** ⑪ as you turn right onto Çadırcı Camii Caddesi, which runs into Fuatpaşa Caddesi. Follow Fuatpaşa Caddesi along the eastern side of the grounds of **Istanbul University** ⑫. Continue along Fuatpaşa Caddesi, keeping the grounds of the university on your left, until the junction with Prof. Sıddık Sami Ona Caddesi and Ismetiye Caddesi. Turn left along Prof. Sıddık Sami Ona Caddesi to **Süleymaniye Cami** ⑬. After visiting this mosque, retrace your steps along Prof. Sıddık Sami Ona Caddesi, continue straight across into Ismetiye Caddesi, and then turn left down Çarşı Caddesi. Along the narrow road leading downhill is a thriving market lined with stalls and small shops selling mostly cheap clothing. Continue down the hill to Hasırcılar Caddesi to head into the **Eminönü** ⑭ neighborhood. The **Rüstem Paşa Cami** ⑮ is at the western edge of this neighborhood. After visiting this mosque, continue along Hasırcılar Caddesi to the **Egyptian Bazaar** ⑯.

TIMING

Not counting the streets of the Grand Bazaar, it takes about an hour to complete this walk. If you spend a brief amount of time in each of the mosques and bazaars and stop for lunch, then it will take you about four or five hours. The Grand and Egyptian bazaars are closed Sunday, though the small Arasta Bazaar in the Sultanahmet neigbhorhood is open. The Beyazıt, Rüstem Paşa, and Süleymaniye mosques are open daily.

Sights to See

⑪ **Beyazıt Cami.** No, your eyes do not deceive you; this domed mosque was also inspired by Aya Sofya. It dates from 1504 and is the oldest of the Ottoman imperial mosques still standing in the city. ⊠ *Beyazıt Meyd., Beyazıt*, ☎ *no phone.* ⌑ *Free.* ☾ *Sunrise to sunset daily, usually closed during prayer times.*

★ ⑯ **Egyptian Bazaar** (Mısır Çarşısı). Also known as the Spice Market, the Egyptian Bazaar is much smaller than the Grand

Bazaar but is still lively and colorful. It was built in the 17th century to generate rental income to pay for the upkeep of the **Yeni Cami** (New Mosque), next door. Once a vast pharmacy filled with burlap bags overflowing with herbs and spices, the bazaar today is chockablock with white sacks of spices, as well as bags full of fruit, nuts, and royal jelly from the beehives of the Aegean Sea. ⊠ *Hamidiye Cad., across from Galata Bridge,* ☎ *no phone.* ☉ *Mon.–Sat. 8–7.*

NEED A
BREAK?

The **Pandelli,** up two flights of stairs over the arched gateway to the Egyptian Bazaar, is a frenetic Old Istanbul restaurant with incredible tiles. A lunch of typical Turkish fare is served; especially good are the eggplant *börek* (pastry) and the sea bass cooked in paper. ⊠ *Mısır Çarşısı 1, Eminönü,* ☎ *212/527-3909. AE, MC, V.*

⑭ Eminönü. The main transportation hub of Old Stamboul, Eminönü is a neighborhood at the south end of the Galata Bridge. It has quays for hydrofoil sea buses, the more traditional Bosporus ferries (including those for the daylong Bosporus cruises), and the Sirkeci train station and tramway terminal. The main coastal road around the peninsula of the old city also traverses Eminönü. Thousands of people and vehicles rush through the bustling area, and numerous street traders here sell everything from candles to live animals.

★ ⑩ **Grand Bazaar** (Kapalı Çarşı). This early version of a shopping mall, also known as the Covered Bazaar, consists of a maze of 65 winding, covered streets crammed with 4,000 tiny shops, cafés, and restaurants. It reputedly has the largest number of stores under one roof anywhere in the world. Originally built by Mehmet II (the Conqueror) in the 1450s, it was ravaged in modern times by two fires—one in 1954 that nearly destroyed it, and a smaller one in 1974. In both cases, the bazaar was quickly rebuilt into something resembling the original style, with arched passageways and brass-and-tile fountains at regular intervals.

It's filled with thousands of items—fabric, clothing (including counterfeit brand names), brass candelabra, furniture, and jewelry. A sizable share of junk tailored for the tourist trade is sold as well. A separate section for antiques at the very center of the bazaar, called the ***bedestan***, is definitely worth checking out. Outside the western gate to the bazaar, through a doorway, is the **Sahaflar Çarşısı**, the Old Book Bazaar, where you can buy both new editions and antique volumes in Turkish and other languages. The best way to explore the bazaar is to take a deep breath and plunge on in. And remember: The best prices are those called out to you when the would-be seller thinks you are about to slip away. ⊠ *Yeniçeriler Cad. and Fuatpaşa Cad.* ▨ *Free.* ☉ *Apr.–Oct., Mon.–Sat. 8:30– 7; Nov.–Mar., Mon.–Sat. 8:30–6:30.*

⑫ **Istanbul University.** The university's magnificent gateway faces Beyazıt Square. The campus, with its long greens and giant plane trees, originally served as the Ottoman war ministry, which helps explain the grandiose, martial style of the portal and the main buildings. In the garden stands the white-marble 200-ft **Beyazıt Tower,** the tallest structure in Old Stamboul, built in 1823 by Mahmut II (ruled 1808–39) as a fire-watch station. ⊠ *Fuat Paşa Cad., Beyazıt.*

⑮ **Rüstem Paşa Cami** (Rüstem Paşa Mosque). This small and often overlooked mosque is another Sinan masterpiece. Tucked away in the backstreets to the north of the Egyptian Bazaar, it was built in the 1550s for Süleyman's grand vizier. Though unassuming from the outside, its interior is decorated with İznik tiles in an array of colors and patterns. ⊠ *Hasırcılar Cad., south of Sobacılar Cad.,* ☏ *no phone.* ☉ *Daily.*

⑬ **Süleymaniye Cami** (Mosque of Süleyman). The grandest and most famous creation of its designer, Sinan, houses his tomb and that of his patron, Süleyman the Magnificent. Its enormous dome is supported by four square columns and arches, and exterior walls buttress smaller domes on either side. The result is a soaring space that gives the impression the dome is held up principally by divine cooperation. Though this is the city's largest mosque, it is less ornate and more spiritual in tone than other imperial mosques. Note the İznik tiles in the *mihrab* (prayer niche). ⊠ *Süleymaniye Cad., near Istanbul University's north gate,* ☏ *no phone.* ☉ *Daily.*

Galata to Taksim

This walk covers the heart of the new town, where the first thing you'll learn is that *new* is a relative term. Much of what you'll see dates from the 19th century—except for the

shops and imported American movies, which are all strictly
20th century. You may find the climb up Karaköy to Tünel
Square tough going. But you can always take the tiny subway from Karaköy to Tünel Square; only 90 seconds, the
trip saves a stiff walk.

A Good Walk

Cross over the **Galata Köprüsü** ⑰, stopping on the bridge to
take in one of the world's great city views. Continue due north
up Karaköy Caddesi and then up some steps near the junction with **Voyvoda Caddesi** ⑱. Go straight up the appropriately named Yüksek Kaldırım Caddesi (Steep Rise Street), lined
with shops selling electronics equipment. Halfway up the hill
is **Galata Kulesi** ⑲; the views from the top of the tower (there
is an elevator) will take away any breath that you may have
left after your steep climb. From Galata Kulesi, continue up
the same road, which is now called Galip Dede Caddesi. Head
up to the **Divan Edebiyatı Müzesi** ⑳, the museum where you
can see the dervishes whirl, and into **Tünel Meydanı** ㉑, the
northern terminus of the minisubway from Karaköy. From
the square a trolley runs along İstiklal Caddesi through
Galatasaray Meydanı ㉒ to **Taksim Meydanı** ㉓. But if you've
made it this far by foot or if you took the subway before, it's
more fun to walk. Stop along the way to have a look at the
Üç Horan Armenian Church, marvel at the many splendid
old buildings lining the street (some now house Western consulates), and browse in the lively flower and fish markets.

TIMING

The time needed for the walk will depend as much on your
stamina as on how long you spend at the sights along the
route. If you are reasonably fit and walk the whole way,
allow from three to four hours. The Galata Kulesi is open
daily. The Divan Edebiyatı Müzesi is closed Monday.

Sights to See

⑳ **Divan Edebiyatı Müzesi** (Divan Literature Museum). Also
called the Galata Mevlevihane, this museum contains costumes, instruments, and memorabilia used by the Sufi mys-
tics known in the West as the whirling dervishes. On the
last Sunday of each month dance performances and Sufi
music concerts are held at 3. ⊠ *Galip Dede Cad. 15, southeast of Tünel Sq., off İstiklal Cad., Beyoğlu,* ☏ *212/245–
4141.* ⌨ *$5.* ☉ *Tues.–Sun. 9:30–4:30.*

★ **⑰** **Galata Köprüsü** (Galata Bridge). The bridge that joins Istanbul's older, European districts to the new town yields one of the world's great city views. In Old Stamboul, behind you as you cross the bridge toward Karaköy, landmarks include Topkapı Palace, the domes and minarets of Aya Sofya and the Blue Mosque, and the Süleymaniye and Yeni mosques. Ferries chug out on the Bosporus, and Galata Tower rises high on the Beyoğlu side of the Golden Horn, beyond Karaköy. The drawbridge that you're standing on opened in 1993, when it replaced the old pontoon bridge that had been around since 1910, in the days when horse-, ox-, or mule-drawn carriages rattled across it for a fee. ⊠ *Sobacılar Cad., in Eminönü, to Rıhtım Cad., in Karaköy.*

⑲ **Galata Kulesi** (Galata Tower). The Genoese built this tower as part of their fortifications in 1349, when they controlled the northern shore of the Golden Horn. In this century the rocket-shape tower served as a fire lookout until 1960. Today it houses a restaurant and nightclub (☞ Nightclubs *in* Chapter 5) and a viewing tower (accessible by elevator) that is open during the day. The area around the Galata Tower was a thriving Italian settlement both before and after the fall of Constantinople. In 1492, when the Spanish Inquisition drove Sephardic Jews from Spain and Portugal, many refugees settled here. For centuries after, a large Jewish population lived in Galata. Although most have moved to the suburbs, they maintain a sense of community in the neighborhood. Today 16 active synagogues, one of which dates from the Byzantine period, serve a Jewish community of 25,000. The **Neve Shalom Synagogue**, on Büyük Hendek Sokak near the Galata Tower, was where 22 Sabbath worshipers were shot by Arabic-speaking gunmen in September 1986. A visit to the now high-security location requires a show of identification. Some older Turkish Jews still speak a dialect of medieval Spanish called Ladino, or Judeo-Spanish. ⊠ *Galata Tower: Büyük Hendek Cad.,* ☏ *212/ 245–1160.* ☞ *$1.* ☉ *Daily 9–8.*

㉒ **Galatasaray Meydanı** (Galatasaray Square). This square is in the heart of the Beyoğlu district. The impressive building behind the massive iron gates on the square is a high school, established in 1868 and for a time the most prestigious in the Ottoman Empire. Across İstiklal Caddesi, at

Number 51, is the entrance to the **Çiçek Pasajı** (Flower Arcade), a lively warren of flower stalls, tiny restaurants, and bars. Street musicians often entertain here. Curmudgeons swear the passage is a pale shadow of its former self—its original neobaroque home collapsed with a thundering crash one night in 1978, and its redone facade and interior feel too much like a reproduction—but you can still get a feel for its bohemian past. Behind the Flower Arcade is the **Balık Pazarı** (Fish Market), a bustling labyrinth of stands peddling fish, fruits, vegetables, and spices—with a couple of pastry shops thrown in—all of which makes for great street theater. The Fish Market is open from Monday through Saturday during daylight hours. At the end of the Fish Market, at Meşrutiyet Caddesi, is the **Üç Horan Armenian Church** (✉ İstiklal Cad. 288). With its crosses and haloed Christs, the church is an unexpected sight in Muslim Istanbul.

İstiklal Caddesi (Independence Street). One of European Istanbul's main thoroughfares heads north and east to Taksim Square from Tünel Square. Consulates in ornate turn-of-the-century buildings and 19th-century apartments line the route, along with bookstores, boutiques, kebab shops, and movie theaters. To appreciate the architecture, look toward the upper stories of what was once the most fashionable street in the entire region. Return your gaze to eye level, and you will see every element of modern Istanbul's vibrant cultural melting pot. A trolley runs along İstiklal every 10 minutes or so, all the way to Taksim Square. The fare is about 50¢. If you have the time and energy, walk one way and take the trolley back.

㉓ Taksim Meydanı (Taksim Square). The square at the north end of İstiklal Caddesi is in the not particularly handsome center of the new town, especially since municipal subway digging turned its belly into a deep concrete crevasse. It's basically a chaotic traffic circle with a bit of grass and the **Monument to the Republic and Independence,** featuring Atatürk and his revolutionary cohorts. Around the square are Istanbul's main concert hall, **Atatürk Kültür Merkezi** (Atatürk Cultural Center), the high-rise Marmara Hotel, and, on a grassy promenade, the 23-story Ceylan Inter-Continental (☞ Chapter 4). On **Cumhuriyet Caddesi,** the main street headed north from the square, are shops selling carpets and leather goods. Also here are the entrances to the Hyatt, Divan, and Istanbul Hilton hotels; several travel agencies and airline ticket offices; and a few nightclubs. Cumhuriyet turns into Halâskârgazi Caddesi. When this street meets Rumeli Caddesi, you enter the city's high-fashion district, where Turkey's top designers sell their wares.

NEED A
BREAK?

The **Patisserie Café Marmara,** in the Marmara Hotel on Taksim Square, serves hot and cold drinks and snacks, ice cream, and excellent homemade cakes. Despite the turbulence and often downright chaos of Taksim Square itself, the café retains an air of unhurried calm. A duo usually plays soothing classical music in the late afternoon or early evening. In summer the shaded terrace is a good place to observe the bustle of the square. ⊠ *Marmara Istanbul, Taksim Sq.,* ☎ *212/251–4696. AE, DC, MC, V.*

㉑ Tünel Meydanı (Tünel Square). The northern terminus of the city's mini-subway is at this square on the south end of İstiklal Caddesi. Nearby is the **Pera Palace,** one of the most famous of Istanbul's hotels, where Agatha Christie wrote *Murder on the Orient Express* and where Mata Hari threw back a few at the bar.

⑱ Voyvoda Caddesi. Considering all the trouble he's said to have caused, it's a tad ironic that the street named after the 15th-century *voyvode* (prince) of Transylvania, Vlad the Impaler—better known as Count Dracula—is a nondescript commercial strip. As a child, Vlad was sent to the Ottoman sultan as ransom, and though he was finally released, he grew up despising the Turks. He devised elaborate tortures for his enemies and at length drove the Turks from Romania. Killed near Bucharest in 1476, his head was sent to Constantinople, where Mehmet II the Conqueror displayed it on a stake to prove to all that the hated Vlad was finally dead. Some say the street is the site of his grave.

OFF THE
BEATEN
PATH

RAHMI KOÇ SANAYI MÜZESI – A restored foundry once used to cast anchors for the Ottoman fleet now houses this industrial museum tracing the development of technology. Exhibits include medieval telescopes and the great engines that powered the Bosporus ferries. A special section devoted to transportation includes planes, bicycles, motorbikes, and some

In case you want to see the world.

At American Express, we're here to make your journey a smooth one. So we have over 1,700 travel service locations in over 120 countries ready to help. What else would you expect from the world's largest travel agency?

do more ®

http://www.americanexpress.com/travel

Travel

In case you want to be welcomed there.

We're here to see that you're always welcomed at establishments everywhere. That's why millions of people carry the American Express® Card – for peace of mind, confidence, and security, around the world or just around the corner.

do more ®

Cards

In case you're running low.

We're here to help with more than 118,000 Express Cash locations around the world. In order to enroll, just call American Express before you start your vacation.

do more

Express Cash

And just in case.

We're here with American Express® Travelers Cheques and Cheques *for Two.*® They're the safest way to carry money on your vacation and the surest way to get a refund, practically anywhere, anytime.
Another way we help you...

do more

AMERICAN EXPRESS

Travelers Cheques

well-crafted maritime instruments. ⊠ *27 Hasköy Cad., Hasköy,* ☎ *212/256-7153 or 212/256-7154,* ℻ *212/ 256-7156.* ▣ *$1.50.* ☉ *Tues.–Sun. 10–5.*

Beşiktaş

The shore of the Bosporus became the favorite residence of the later Ottoman sultans as they sought to escape over-crowded Old Stamboul. They remained here until the end of the empire when eventually they, too, were engulfed by the ever-expanding city and, one could argue, by history as well.

A Good Walk

Start at the extravagant 19th-century **Dolmabahçe Sarayı** ㉔, the palace where the last sultans of the Ottoman Empire resided and where Atatürk then lived. Exiting the palace, continue northeast along tree-lined Dolmabahçe Caddesi onto Beşiktaş Caddesi, site of the **Deniz Müzesi** ㉕, to get a sense of the Ottoman Empire's former naval power. From here follow the main coast road past the Beşiktaş ferry terminal into Çırağan Caddesi and the **Çırağan Sarayı** ㉖, former home of the Sultan Abdül Aziz and now a luxury hotel. Directly opposite the hotel's main door is the entrance to the wooded slopes of **Yıldız Parkı** ㉗, probably the most romantic spot in Istanbul. Follow the road up the hill through the park and take a right at the top of the slope to get to Yıldız Şale, the chalet of the last of the Ottoman sultans.

TIMING

Allow approximately two hours from leaving Dolmabahçe Sarayı to the entrance to Yıldız Parkı, including 45 minutes in the Deniz Müzesi (Naval Museum) and 30 minutes in the Çırağan Sarayı. Allow another two to three hours to walk through Yıldız Parkı—it has numerous trails—and include 45 minutes to an hour to visit Yıldız Şale. Dolmabahçe Sarayı is closed Monday and Thursday, as is the Naval Museum. Yıldız Parkı is open daily, but Yıldız Şale is closed Monday and Tuesday.

Sights to See

❷❻ **Çırağan Sarayı** (Çırağan Palace). Istanbul's most luxurious hotel (☞ Chapter 4) was built by Abdül Mecit's brother and successor, Sultan Abdül Aziz (ruled 1861–76), in 1863. That the palace is about a third the size of Dolmabahçe and much less ornate says a good deal about the declining state of the Ottoman Empire's coffers. The vacuous Abdül Aziz was as extravagant as his brother and was soon attempting to emulate the splendors he had seen on travels in England and France. Today the restored grounds, with a splendid swimming pool at the edge of the Bosporus, are worth a look, and the hotel bar provides a plush, cool respite with a view. You won't find much from the original palace, as a major fire gutted the place; the lobby renovations were done with a nod to the palace's original 19th-century design, though the color scheme is decidedly gaudier. ⊠ Çırağan Cad. 84, Beşiktaş, ☎ 212/258–3377.

㉕ Deniz Müzesi (Naval Museum). The Ottoman Empire was the 16th century's leading sea power. The flashiest displays here are the sultan's barges, the long, slim boats that served as the primary mode of royal transportation for several hundred years. The museum's cannon collection includes a 23-ton blaster built for Sultan Selim the Grim. An early Ottoman map of the New World, cribbed from Columbus, dates from 1513. ⊠ Beşiktaş Cad., ☎ 212/261–0040 or 212/261–0130. ⊡ $1. ⊙ Fri.– Sun. and Tues.–Wed. 9–noon and 1:30–5.

㉔ Dolmabahçe Sarayı (Dolmabahçe Palace). The last sultans of the Ottoman Empire resided at this palace, erected in 1853. After the establishment of the modern republic in 1923, it became the home of Atatürk, who died here in 1938. The name, which means "filled-in garden," predates the palace; Sultan Ahmet I (ruled 1603–17) had a little cove filled in and an imperial garden planted here in the 17th century. The palace is an extraordinary mixture of Hindu, Turkish, and European styles of architecture and interior design. Abdül Mecit, whose free-spending lifestyle (his main distinction) eventually bankrupted his empire, intended the structure to be a symbol of Turkey's march away from its past and toward the European mainstream. He gave his Armenian architect, Balian, complete freedom and an unlimited budget. His only demand was that the palace "surpass any other palace of any other potentate anywhere in the world."

The result was a riot of rococo—marble, vast mirrors, stately towers, and formal gardens along a facade stretching nearly ½ km (⅓ mi). His bed was solid silver; the tub and basins in his marble-paved bathroom were carved of translucent alabaster. Europe's royalty contributed to the splendor: Queen Victoria sent a chandelier weighing 4½ tons, Czar Nicholas I of Russia provided polar-bear rugs. The result is as gaudy and showy as a palace should be, all gilt and crystal and silk, and every bit as garish as Versailles. The nearby **Dolmabahçe Cami** (Dolmabahçe Mosque) was founded in 1853 by Abdül Mecit's mother. You must join a guided tour that takes about 80 minutes or a shorter one that takes about 45 minutes and omits the harem. ⊠ *Dolmabahçe Cad.,* ☎ *212/258−5544.* 🎫 *$10 for long tour, $5.50 for short tour.* ☉ *Tues.−Wed. and Fri.−Sun. 9−4.*

㉗ Yıldız Parkı. The wooded slopes of Yıldız Park once formed part of the great forest that covered the European shore of the Bosporus from the Golden Horn to the Black Sea. During the reign of Abdül Aziz, the park was his private garden, and the women of the harem would occasionally be allowed to visit. First the gardeners would be removed, then the eunuchs would lead the women across the wooden bridge from the palace and along the avenue to the upper gardens. Secluded from prying eyes, they would sit in the shade or wander through the acacias, maples, and cypresses, filling their baskets with flowers and figs. Today the park is still hauntingly beautiful, particularly in spring and fall.

Yıldız Şale (Yıldız Chalet), at the top of the park, is yet another palace of Sultan Abdül Hamit II (ruled 1876−1909). Visiting dignitaries from Kaiser Wilhelm to Charles de Gaulle and Margaret Thatcher have stayed here. The chalet is often blissfully empty of other tourists, which makes a visit all the more pleasurable. Forgotten is the turmoil of the era when the palace was occupied by the last rulers of the once-great Ottoman Empire. All were deposed: freespending Abdül Aziz; his unfortunate nephew, Murad (who, having spent most of his life in the harem, was none too sound of mind); and Abdül Hamid, who distinguished himself as the last despot of the Ottoman Empire. ⊠ *Çırağan Cad.,* ☎ *212/261−8460 for park, 212/258−3080 for chalet.* 🎫 *Park: 25¢ pedestrians, $1.50 cars; chalet: $1.50.* ☉ *Park: daily 9−9; chalet: Wed.−Sun. 9−4.*

The Bosporus

Though there are good roads along both the Asian and the European shores, the most pleasant way to explore the Bosporus is by ferry from the Eminönü docks in the old town (☞ Public Transportation *in* Essential Information). Along the way you will see wooded hills, villages large and small, modern and old-fashioned, and the old wooden summer homes called *yalıs* (waterside houses) that were built for the city's wealthier residents in the Ottoman era. When looking at ferry schedules, remember that *Rumeli* refers to the European side, *Anadolu* to the Asian.

A Good Ferry Tour

Numbers in the text correspond to numbers in the margin and on the Bosporus map. There are two ways to take a ferry tour of the Bosporus. One is to take one of the cruises that depart daily from Eminönü. These zigzag up the Bosporus, stop for a couple of hours near the Black Sea for lunch, then zigzag back down to Eminönü. The other way is to fashion your own tour, hopping on one of the regular Bosporus commuter ferries, stopping wherever you fancy, and then continuing your journey on the next ferry going your way. (Buy a ferry timetable—a *vapur tarifesi*—to figure out your itinerary.) The advantage of the latter is more freedom; the disadvantage is that you will probably end up spending considerable extra time waiting for the next ferry. Note, too, that not all ferries stop at every quay along the Bosporus, and during the middle of the day schedules can be erratic.

After departing from Eminönü, the ferry heads north out of the Golden Horn and past the Dolmabahçe and Çırağan palaces on the European shore. As you approach the first Bosporus bridge you pass Ortaköy Cami (Ortaköy Mosque) on the European shore and, just past the bridge on the Asian shore, the **Beylerbeyi Sarayı** ㉘. Back on the European side is the village of **Arnavutköy** ㉙, followed by the stylish suburb of **Bebek** ㉚. Just before the second Bosporus bridge (officially known as Fatih Sultan Mehmet Bridge) are two fortresses, **Anadolu Hisarı** ㉛, on the Asian side, and **Rumeli Hisarı** ㉜, on the European side. North of Fatih Sultan Mehmet Bridge, on the Asian side, lies the village of **Kanlıca** ㉝. Across the water are the wooded slopes of **Emirgan** ㉞. Still farther north on the European side are the fashionable resort area of Tarabya and the waterfront village of Sarıyer, the ferry stop for the **Sadberk Hanım Müzesi** ㉟, with its collection of Islamic and Turkish arts and Anatolian archaeological finds. Organized cruises from Eminönü usually stop at either Rumeli Kavag̉ı or Anadolu Kavağı, two fishing villages, for a couple of hours. Anadolu Kavağı is particularly fun; its sidewalk vendors sell deep-fried mussels and sweet waffles. The ferries begin their return trips to Istanbul from Rumeli Kavağı and Anadolu Kavağı.

TIMING

Whether you take a Bosporus cruise or make your own way by ferry, you should allow a whole day. The cruises usually take about six hours. Add at least an extra hour (if not longer) for waiting for ferries in addition to the time spent at stops along the way. Rumeli Hisarı is closed Monday. Beylerbeyi Sarayı is closed Monday and Thursday. Sadberk Hanım Müzesi is closed Wednesday.

Sights to See

㉛ **Anadolu Hisarı** (Anatolian Castle). Sultan Beyazıt I built this fortress in 1393 to cut off Constantinople's access to the Black Sea. At the mouth of the Göksu stream, known in Ottoman times as one of the "Sweet Waters of Asia," the castle is a romantic sight (especially at sunset). Its golden stone blends into the surrounding forest, and tiny boats bob beneath its walls (some of which are crumbling, so be careful if walking on them). An unmarked path leads up to the castle ruins; there's no admission fee.

㉙ **Arnavutköy.** This village on the European side of the Bosporus has a row of 19th-century wooden houses at the water's edge. Up the hill from the water, narrow streets contain more old wooden houses, some of them with trailing vines.

㉚ **Bebek.** One of the most fashionable suburbs of Istanbul, particularly with an affluent expatriate community, Bebek has a shaded park on the waterfront next to the mosque, good restaurants and open-air cafés, and a jazz club. Small rowing boats and even sizable cutters with crew can be rented for trips around Bebek Bay.

㉘ **Beylerbeyi Sarayı** (Beylerbeyi Palace). Built for Sultan Abdül Aziz in 1865, Beylerbeyi is a mini-Dolmabahçe,

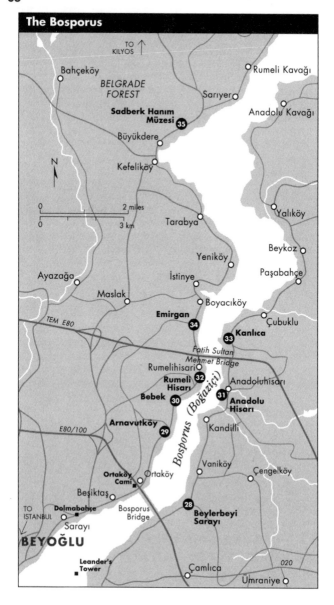

The Bosporus

TO KILYOS ↑

Bahçeköy

Rumeli Kavağı

BELGRADE FOREST

Sarıyer

Anadolu Kavağı

Sadberk Hanım Müzesi 35

Büyükdere

N

Kefeliköy

0 ——— 2 miles
0 ——— 3 km

Tarabya

Yalıköy

Beykoz

Yeniköy

Paşabahçe

Ayazağa

İstinye

Maslak

Boyacıköy

Emirgan 34

Çubuklu

TEM E80

Kanlıca 33

Fatih Sultan Mehmet Bridge

Rumelihisarı

Rumeli Hisarı 32

Anadoluhisarı

Bebek 30

31

Anadolu Hisarı

E80/100

Arnavutköy 29

Kandilli

Bosporus (Boğaziçi)

Vaniköy

Çengelköy

Ortaköy Cami

Ortaköy

Beşiktaş

TO ISTANBUL

Dolmabahçe ■

Bosporus Bridge

28

Beylerbeyi Sarayı

Sarayı

BEYOĞLU

Leander's Tower ■

Çamlıca

020

Ümraniye

filled with marble and marquetry and gold-encrusted furniture. The central hall has a white-marble fountain and a
stairway wide enough for a regiment. You must join a tour
to see the palace. ⊠ *Çayıbaşı Durağı, Beylerbeyi,* ☎ *216/
321–9320.* ⊑ *$3.* ☉ *Tues.–Wed. and Fri.–Sun. 9:30–5.*

㉞ Emirgan. This town on the European shore of the Bosporus
was named after a 17th-century Persian prince to whom Sultan Murat IV (ruled 1623–40) presented a palace here. The
woods above are part of a park with flower gardens and a
number of restored Ottoman pavilions. In late April the
town stages a Tulip Festival. Tulips take their name from the
Turkish *tulbend* (turban); the flowers were originally brought
from Mongolia, and after their cultivation was refined by
the Dutch, they were great favorites of the Ottoman sultans.

㉝ Kanlıca. White 19th-century wooden villas line the waterfront of this village on the Asian shore. Kanlıca has been
famous for its delicious yogurt for at least 300 years; it's
served in little restaurants around the plane tree in the
square by the quay.

㉜ Rumeli Hisarı (Thracian Castle). Mehmet the Conqueror built
this eccentric-looking fortress in 1452, a year before his siege
of Constantinople finally succeeded. Its crenellated walls
and round towers are popular with photographers, though
what you see from the water is about all there is to see. In
summer Rumeli Hisarı is sometimes used for Shakespeare
performances (usually in Turkish) and music and folk dancing. ⊠ *Rumeli Hisarı Cad.,* ☎ *no phone.* ⊑ *$1.* ☉ *Tues.–
Sun. 9:30–5.*

㉟ Sadberk Hanım Müzesi (Sadberk Hanım Museum). An old
waterfront mansion houses this museum named for the de-
ceased wife of the late billionaire businessman Vehbi Koç.
Though small, it houses an enviable collection of high-
quality pieces. Half of the museum is dedicated to Islamic
and Turkish arts (from İznik tiles to Ottoman embroidery
and calligraphy), and half to Anatolian archaeology (Hittite pottery and cuneiform tablets). ⊠ *Piyasa Cad. 27–29,
Büyükdere,* ☎ *212/242–3813.* ⊑ *$2.* ☉ *Apr.–Oct.,
Thurs.–Tues. 10:30–6; Nov.–Mar., Thurs.–Tues. 10–5.*

3 Dining

TURKEY IS NOT JUST a geographic bridge linking Europe, Asia, and the Middle East; it's a gastronomic one as well. Its cuisine reflects the history of a people who emigrated from the borders of China to a land mass known as Asia Minor and built an empire that encompassed Arab, Asian, and European lands.

Istanbul has a range of restaurants—and prices to match. Most major hotels serve standard international cuisine, so it's more rewarding to eat in Turkish restaurants. Beer, wine, and sometimes cocktails are widely available despite Muslim proscriptions against alcohol. Dress is casual unless otherwise noted.

The price categories in the listings below refer to the chart in On the Road with Fodor's. For more about dining in Istanbul and Turkish cuisine, *see* Essential Information, and Pleasures and Pastimes in Chapter 1.

Asian Shore

$$$$ ✕ **Reşat Paşa Konağı.** A chic atmosphere prevails inside this pink-and-white gingerbread-style villa. It's a little out of the way, on the Asian side, but the delicious Ottoman and Turkish dishes are well worth the trip (which you can make with a taxi driver instructed by someone at your hotel). Order à la carte and sample the mixed seafood cooked in a clay pot, or let the waiter tempt you with the *Paşa Sofrasi*, a fixed-priced menu that includes 20 cold and hot appetizers, shish kebab as a main course, and lemon *helva* (halvah) for dessert, all accompanied by unlimited domestic drinks. A band plays *fasil* (traditional Turkish music) on weekends. ⊠ *Sinan Ercan Cad. 34/1, Kozyatağı Mah., Erenköy,* ☎ *216/361–3411 or 216/361–3487. AE, DC, V. Closed Mon. No lunch.*

South of the Golden Horn

$$$ ✕ **Develi Restaurant.** One of the oldest and best kebab
★ restaurants in Istanbul also has great views across the Sea of Marmara. The specialty is dishes from southeast Ana-

40

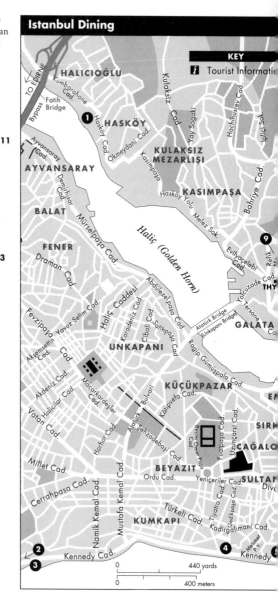

Istanbul Dining

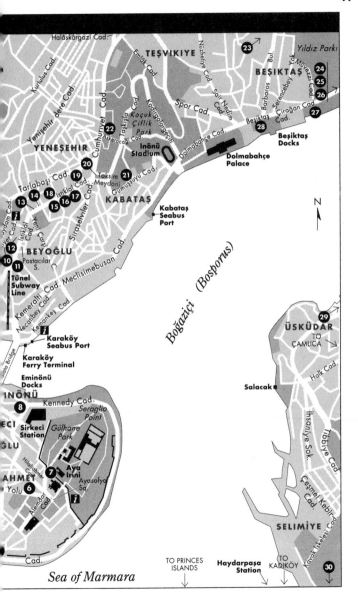

tolia, which are traditionally more spicy than those in the west of the country. Try the *patlıcan kebap* (kebab with eggplant) or the *fıstıklı kebap* (kebab with pistachios). ✉ *Balıkpazarı, Gümüşyüzük Sok. 7, Samatya,* ☎ *212/585–1189 or 212/529–0833. AE, DC, MC, V.*

$$$ ✕ **Gelik.** In a two-story 19th-century villa, this restaurant is usually packed with people savoring its delicious specialty: all types of meat roasted in deep cooking wells to produce rich, unusual stews. ✉ *Sahilyolu 68–70,* ☎ *212/560–7284. AE, DC, MC, V.*

$$$ ✕ **Sarniç.** It's not often you get to dine deep down in an old Roman cistern. Candlelight reflects off the arched yellow-brick walls, and a large fireplace provides warmth in chilly weather. The service is fairly formal, and the fare is a mix of Turkish and Continental, ranging from duck à l'orange to *döner kebap* (meat roasted on a spit). ✉ *Sogukçesme Sok., Sultanahmet,* ☎ *212/512–4291. AE, V.*

$$ ✕ **Borsa Lokantasi.** This unpretentious spot with func-
★ tional furnishings is usually filled with a crowd of hungry Turks who have come to eat some great, reasonably priced food. The baked lamb in eggplant puree and the stuffed artichokes are especially good. ✉ *Yalıköşkü Cad., Yalıköşkü Han 60–62, Eminönü,* ☎ *212/522–4173. No credit cards.*

$$ ✕ **Fırat.** At this hopping Kumkapı fish house, you barely have time to settle in before food starts coming at you: salads, a savory baked liver dish, shrimp with garlic. In addition to the usual grilled presentations, fish here is baked in a light cream- or tomato-based sauce to great effect. Just point at what you want, but try to save room for dessert. ✉ *Çakmaktaş Sok. 11, Kumkapı,* ☎ *212/517–2308. AE, MC, V.*

$ ✕ **Doy-Doy.** "Doy-doy" is a Turkish expression for "full," and you can indeed fill up here for a reasonable sum. Kebabs, *pide* (Turkish pizza), and mezes are served. If you're a vegetarian, the meatless pizzas and salad are good options. Service is friendly, and the menu's prices are unambiguous (sometimes a problem in Istanbul). ✉ *Şifa Hamamı Sok. 13, Sultanahmet,* ☎ *212/517–1588. No credit cards.*

$ ✕ **Tarihi Sultanahmet Köftecisi.** Although a number of branches exist across the city, this one is the original home of Sultanahmet *köfte* (meatballs). This restaurant has built a small empire from a combination of bare, almost austere decor and an even simpler menu, which has remained virtually unchanged for more than 75 years—meatballs, *piyaz* (boiled white beans in olive oil), and salad. Its location, a couple of minutes' walk from the Blue Mosque and Aya Sofya, makes it ideal for a quick lunch. ⊠ *Divan Yolu 12, Sultanahmet,* ☎ *212/513–1438. No credit cards.*

Beyoğlu Area

$$ ✕ **Çatı.** This restaurant on a Beyoğlu side street serves hot and cold Turkish dishes and a good buffet. It's on the seventh floor, which allows you to appreciate the architectural splendors of İstiklal Caddesi. Before perusing the menu, ask the waiter about the day's specials. It's open late, and often live music is performed in the evenings. ⊠ *Orhan Apaydın Sok. 20/7, İstiklal Cad., Beyoğlu,* ☎ *212/251–0000. MC, V. Closed Sun.*

$$ ✕ **Dört Mevsim** (Four Seasons). A handsome Victorian build-
★ ing on the new town's main drag houses this restaurant, noted for its blend of Turkish and French cuisine. Opened in 1965 by an Anglo-Turkish couple, Gay and Musa, today you'll still find them in the kitchen overseeing the preparation of such delights as shrimp in cognac sauce and baked marinated lamb. ⊠ *İstiklal Cad. 509, Beyoğlu,* ☎ *212/293–3941 or 212/243–6320. DC, MC, V. Closed Sun.*

$$ ✕ **Osmancık.** On the 23rd floor of the Mercure Hotel, this Turkish restaurant has a 360-degree view of the Bosporus, the Golden Horn, and the rest of Istanbul. The fixed-price menu includes appetizers such as *osmancık boreği* (cheese-filled pastries topped with a yogurt sauce) and grills and all the domestic liquors you want to drink. Entertainment, which starts after 9 PM, comes in the form of traditional Turkish music, followed by a belly dancer. ⊠ *Meşrutiyet Cad., Tepebaşı,* ☎ *212/251–5074. AE, DC, MC, V.*

$$ ✕ **Rejans.** After a few years when it appeared to be sliding into decay, the Rejans has a new lease on life. Established by Russian émigrés who fled the Bolshevik revolution, the restaurant is now run by their widows. In the 1930s and 1940s it was one of Istanbul's premier restaurants. Plaques on the wall bear witness to the famous and infamous who once dined here, from statesmen to World War II spies and diplomats. Despite a fresh coat of paint, the decor has remained basically unchanged since the restaurant's heyday, and live Russian music from an accordion-led trio is performed on the balcony Thursday–Saturday. The excellent range of appetizers includes piroshki and borscht, and main courses highlight beef Stroganoff, chicken Kiev, and pork chops. ⊠ *Emir Nevrut Sok. 17, İstiklal Cad., Beyoğlu,* ☎ *212/244–1610. Reservations essential Fri. and Sat. DC, MC, V. Closed Sun.*

$$ ✕ **Zindan.** Two hundred years ago this Ottoman *meyhane* (tavern) was a prison. Today it is a popular haunt of Turk-ish intellectuals and businesspeople, drawn by its superb tra-ditional Turkish cuisine and its atmosphere, created by live *fasıl* (Turkish classical) music. ⊠ *İstiklal Caddesi, Olivai Han Geçidi 13, Galatasaray,* ☎ *212/252–7340. DC, MC, V.*

$ ✕ **Hacı Abdullah.** Authentic, inexpensive traditional Ot-toman and Turkish cuisine has made this a favorite for lo-cals wishing to enjoy good food in a relaxed atmosphere without loud music or alcohol. The restaurant is famous for its appetizers, grilled meats, and seemingly inexhaustible range of pickles and homemade fruit compotes. ⊠ *Ağa Camii Sakızağacı Cad. 17, Beyoğlu,* ☎ *212/293–8561. No credit cards.*

$ ✕ **Hacı Salih.** You may have to line up for lunch at this tiny,
★ family-run restaurant—it has only 10 tables. But the tra-ditional Turkish fare is worth the wait. Lamb and vegetable dishes are specialties, and though alcohol is not served, you are welcome to bring your own. ⊠ *Anadolu Han 201/1–2, off Alyon Sok. (off İstiklal Cad.),* ☎ *212/243–4528. MC, V. Closed Sun. No dinner.*

$ ✕ **Hacıbaba.** The menu at this large, cheerful place runs the gamut of Turkish specialties; the lamb kebabs are good, and there are so many mezes that you may never get around to ordering main courses. The shady terrace overlooks a Greek Orthodox churchyard. ⊠ *İstiklal Cad. 49, Taksim,* ☎ *212/244–1886 or 212/245–4377. AE, MC, V.*

$ ✕ **Nature and Peace.** One of the increasing number of health food restaurants opening in Istanbul, this small eatery serves a range of vegetarian and healthy dishes in a nostalgic, turn-of-the-century atmosphere. ⊠ *Büyükparmakkapı Sokak 21, Beyoğlu,* ☎ *212/252–8609. AE, MC, V. Closed Sun.*

$ ✕ **Yakup 2.** This cheery hole-in-the-wall is smoky and filled with locals rather than tourists. It can get loud, es-pecially if there is a soccer match on the television. From the stuffed peppers to the octopus salad, the mezes are several notches above average. ⊠ *Asmalı Mescit Cad. 35–37,* ☎ *212/249–2925. AE, V.*

$ ✕ **Zencefil.** The menu at this pioneering vegetarian restaurant, one of the first to open in Istanbul, changes daily. But it usually includes the house specialty, mushrooms with potatoes, as well as excellent homemade breads and salads. The atmosphere is intimate and café-like. ⊠ *Kurabiye Sok. 3, Beyoğlu,* ☎ *212/244–4082. No credit cards. Closed Sun.*

Hasköy

$$$$ ✕ **Café du Levant.** Black-and-white floor tiles and turn-of-the century European furnishings give this café next to the Rahmi Koç Industrial Museum the feel of a Paris bistro. Chefs Giles and Cyril make superb French cuisine, including fillet of turbot with zucchini and tomatoes. For dessert try the crème brûlée or the orange cake with ice cream. ⊠ *27 Hasköy Cad., Hasköy,* ☎ *212/250–8938 or 212/256–7163. Reservations essential. AE, DC, MC, V. Closed Mon.*

Taksim Square Area

$$$ ✕ **Divan.** The Divan, in the hotel of the same name, is a rare exception to the rule to avoid hotel restaurants. The menu is a thoughtful blend of Turkish and French cuisine, the surroundings are elegant, and the service is excellent. ⊠ *In the Divan Hotel, Cumhuriyet Cad. 2, Beyoğlu,* ☎ *212/231–4100. AE, DC, MC. Closed Sun.*

$$ ✕ **Ayaspaşa Russian Restaurant.** Once run by Russians and now managed by Turks, the menu and ambience at this restaurant leave little doubt as to its origins. Tapes of Russian folk songs play in the background, and borscht, lemon vodka, and chicken Kiev are served. The beef Stroganoff is also excellent, as are the consistently tasty pork chops. ⊠ *İnönü Cad. 77/A, Gümüşuyu, Taksim,* ☎ *212/243–4892. MC, V.*

$ ✕ **Sütiş.** This unpretentious spot on the edge of Taksim Square never seems to close. Its cramped frontage opens into a spacious two-tiered interior where the clientele changes with the hours, from office workers eating cheese- or ground-beef-filled börek before work to shoppers and students chatting over tea or a light lunch to bleary-eyed, late-night revelers enjoying Turkish coffee and milk pudding before beginning the journey home. ⊠ *Sıraselviler Cad. 9/4, Taksim,* ☎ *212/252–9204. No credit cards.*

Etiler

$$$ ✕ **Home Store.** On the ground floor of the Akmerkez shopping mall, in the shop of the same name, Home Store doubles as a bar for the Turkish yuppies spilling out of the offices in the surrounding business district. But the food—whether you come for lunch or an early dinner (it closes at 10 PM)—is very good. The menu includes a range of salads, meat and vegetable dishes, superb soups, and desserts. ⊠ *Akmerkez, Etiler,* ☎ *212/282–0253. MC, V.*

The Bosporus

$$$$ ✕ **Körfez.** Call ahead and this restaurant in the picturesque Asian village of Kanlıca can arrange to have you ferried across the Bosporus from Rumeli Hisar. The look is nautical, and the seafood fresh and superbly cooked to order; sample such dishes as flying-fish chowder, and sea bass cooked in salt. ⊠ *Körfez Cad. 78, Kanlıca,* ☎ *216/413–4314. Reservations essential. AE, DC, MC, V. Closed Mon.*

$$$$ ✕ **Tuğra.** In the Çırağan Palace, this spacious and luxurious restaurant serves the most delectable of long-lost and savored Ottoman recipes, including stuffed bluefish and Circassian chicken. Cookbooks from the Ottoman palace were used to re-create some of the dishes. But that's not all: The Bosporus view is flanked by the palace's marble columns, and ornate glass chandeliers hover above, all making you feel like royalty. ⊠ *Çırağan Cad. 84,* ☎ *212/258–3377. Reservations essential. Jacket required. AE, DC, MC, V. No lunch.*

$$$$ ✕ **Ulus 29.** Seafood is the specialty of this chic restaurant, serving an "in" crowd. During the spring, fall, and winter, it's in the suburb of Etiler; in summer it's on the Asian side of the Bosporus. The Etiler location is all silver and crystal and candlelight; the Asian premises recall a Roman villa, except for the view of the yachts bobbing in the harbor. After midnight dancing gets going upstairs in both locations and continues until 2 AM. The place can be pretty dead when

the weather gets cold, however. ⊠ *Akatlar Parkı, Ulus, Etiler,* ☎ *212/265–6181 or 212/265–6198 in spring, fall, and winter;* ⊠ *Paşabahçe Yolu, Çubuklu,* ☎ *216/322– 2829 in summer. Reservations essential. Jacket required. AE, DC, MC, V. No lunch on weekends in summer.*

$$ ✕ **A la Turka.** This cozy little restaurant in the Bohemian quarter of Ortaköy serves excellent *mantı* (Turkish ravioli), *gözleme* (meat-, cheese-, or spinach-stuffed phyllo pastry), köfte, and a large range of salads, but no alcohol. In summer outdoor seating is available. ⊠ *Hazine Sok. 8, Ortaköy,* ☎ *212/258–7924. MC, V.*

$$ ✕ **Dünya.** Right on the Bosporus in bustling Ortaköy, this restaurant has a view of the Bosporus Bridge, the Ortaköy Mosque, and many a passing boat. But as wonderful as these sights are, the food, such as fresh and delicious appetizers of eggplant or octopus salad, is even better. Ask for a table on the terrace as close to the water as possible. ⊠ *Salhane Sok. 10, Ortaköy,* ☎ *212/258–6385. MC, V.*

$$ ✕ **Hanedan.** The emphasis here is on kebabs—all kinds, all of them excellent. The mezes—tabbouleh, hummus, and the flaky pastries known as *böreks*—are tastier than elsewhere. Crisp white linens set off the cool, dark decor. Tables by the front windows offer the advantage of a view of the lively Beşiktaş Ferry terminal. ⊠ *Çiğdem Sok. 27, Beşiktaş,* ☎ *212/260–4854. AE, MC, V.*

4 Lodging

ALMOST EVERYTHING that you probably want to see in Istanbul is in the older part of town, but the big modern hotels are mainly around Taksim Square in the new town and along the Bosporus, a 15- or 20-minute cab ride away. The Aksaray, Laleli, Sultanahmet, and Beyazıt areas have more modest hotels and family-run *pansiyons* (guest houses). The trade-off for the simpler quarters is convenience: Staying here makes it easy to return to your hotel at midday or to change before dinner. No matter where you stay, plan ahead: Istanbul has a chronic shortage of beds.

The price categories in the listings below refer to the chart in On the Road with Fodor's. For more about accommodations in Istanbul, *see* Essential Information, and Pleasures and Pastimes in Chapter 1.

South of the Golden Horn

$$$$ ★   **Armada Hotel.** Only 10 minutes' walk from Istanbul's main tourist sites, the Armada is a good choice. Rooms are spacious and comfortable and have either sea or old city views. One of the hotel's best views is from the terrace of the Ahırkapı restaurant at night. ⊠ *Ahırkapı, 34400,* ☎ *212/638–1370,* 🕿 *212/518–5060. 110 rooms with bath. 3 restaurants, bar, room service. AE, MC, V.*

$$$$ ★   **Four Seasons Hotel.** A former Turkish prison, this elegant hotel became one of Istanbul's premier accommodations the instant it opened in September 1996. This neoclassical building is only steps from Topkapı Palace and the Aya Sofya. Rooms and suites overlook either the Sea of Marmara or an interior courtyard and are luxuriously outfitted with reading chairs, original works of art, and tiled bathrooms with deep tubs. The glass-enclosed courtyard restaurant serves both international cuisine and local specialties. Service overall is exceptional. ⊠ *Tevkifhane Sok. 1, Sultanahmet, 34490,* ☎ *212/638–8200,* 🕿 *212/ 638–8210. 65 rooms with bath. Restaurant, bar, room service, health club, business services. AE, DC, MC, V.*

Alp Guest House, **12**

Armada Hotel, **8**

Ayasofia Pansiyons, **15**

Berk Guest House, **10**

Büyük Londra, **21**

Büyük Tarabya, **29**

Celal Sultan, **16**

Ceylan Inter-Continental, **23**

Çırağan Palace, **30**

Conrad International İstanbul, **28**

Divan Hotel, **24**

Four Seasons Hotel, **14**

Fehmi Bey, **6**

Galata Residence, **18**

Hotel Barin, **2**

Hotel Empress Zoë, **9**

Hotel Nomade, **7**

Hotel Zürich, **3**

Hyatt Regency, **25**

Ibrahim Paşa Oteli, **5**

Istanbul Hilton, **26**

Kybele, **17**

Mavi Ev, **13**

Merit Antique Hotel, **1**

Pera Palace, **19**

Pierre Loti, **4**

Richmond Hotel, **20**

Sed Hotel, **22**

Swissôtel Istanbul, **27**

Yeşil Ev, **11**

TEŞVİKİYE

BEŞİKTAŞ

Yıldız Parkı

28

29

30

Spor Cad.

27

Beşiktaş Docks

Yenişehir dere Cad.

26

25

24

23

Koçuk Çiflik Park

İnönü Stadium

Dolmabahçe Cad.

Dolmabahçe Palace

YENEŞEHİR

Cumhuriyet Cad.

Tarlabaşı Cad.

İstiklal Cad.

Taksim Meydanı

Gümüşsuyu Cad.

22

KABATAŞ

Kabataş Seabus Port

Sıraselviler Cad.

i

21

20

BEYOĞLU

Postacılar S.

Meclisimebusan Cad.

Tünel Subway Line

18

Kemeraltı Cad.

Necatibey Cad.

Kemankeş Cad.

i

Karaköy Seabus Port

Karaköy Ferry Terminal

Eminönü Docks

Boğaziçi (Bosporus)

ÜSKÜDAR

TO ÇAMLICA

Halk Cad.

Salacak

İhsaniye Sok.

Tıbbiye Cad.

Çeşmei Kebir Cad.

MİNÖNÜ

Kennedy Cad.

Seraglio Point

KECİ

Sirkeci Station

Gülhane Park

ĞLU

Ankara Cad.

Hüdavendigar

17

AHMET

Alemdar Cad.

16

15

Aya İrini

Ayasofya Sq.

i

Yolu

14

5   6

7

11   13

9   10

SELİMİYE

Kavak İskelesi Cad.

8

Cad.

N

Sea of Marmara

TO PRINCES ISLANDS

Haydarpaşa Station

TO KADIKÖY

$$$ 🏨 **Ayasofia Pansiyons.** These guest houses are part of a proj-
ect undertaken by Turkey's Touring and Automobile Club
to restore a little street of 19th-century wooden houses along
the outer wall of Topkapı Palace. One house has been con-
verted into a library and the rest into pansiyons, furnished
in late Ottoman style with Turkish carpets and kilims,
brass beds, and big armoires. Front rooms have a view of
Aya Sofya, but the rest do not; so if you want a view, spec-
ify when you reserve. In summer, tea and refreshments are
served in the small courtyard. ⊠ *Soğukçeşme Sok., Sul-
tanahmet, 34400,* ☎ *212/513–3660,* 🖷 *212/513–3669.
57 rooms with bath. Restaurant, bar, café, Turkish bath.
AE, MC, V.*

$$$ 🏨 **Mavi Ev** (Blue House Hotel). In the heart of the old city,
this hotel has an eccentric blue wood facade and clean but
slightly dowdily decorated rooms with a 1950s feel. Its
rooftop terrace restaurant offers a stunning panorama
across the Bosporus and Sea of Marmara and, particularly
at night when it is floodlighted, a breathtaking view of the
Blue Mosque. ⊠ *Dalbastı Sok. 14, Sultanahmet, 34490,*
☎ *212/638–9010,* 🖷 *212/638–9017. 27 rooms with bath.
3 restaurants, 2 bars. AE, MC, V.*

$$$ 🏨 **Merit Antique Hotel.** Four turn-of-the-century apart-
ment buildings were combined to create this hotel. Rooms
are generic and unimpressive, but the public spaces could-
n't be grander, with arched-glass canopies and reproduc-
tion furnishings in turn-of-the-century style. There's even
a small stream stocked with goldfish running through the
lobby. The only drawback is the neighborhood, on the old-
town side, which is mostly full of cheap hotels and restau-
rants. ⊠ *Ordu Cad. 226, Laleli, 34470,* ☎ *212/513–9300,*
🖷 *212/512–6390. 275 rooms with bath. 4 restaurants, bar,
pool, health club. AE, MC, V.*

$$$ 🏨 **Yeşil Ev** (Green House). Another Touring and Auto-
★   mobile Club project, this one is around the corner from the
Ayasofia Pansiyons. The location is spectacular, on the
edge of a small park between the Blue Mosque and Aya
Sofya. The hotel is decorated in Ottoman style, with lace
curtains and latticed shutters; rooms have brass beds and
carved wooden furniture upholstered in velvet or silk (but
they're small, with smallish baths and no phones or tele-
visions). ⊠ *Kabasakal Cad. 5, Sultanahmet, 34400,* ☎

212/517–6785, FAX *212/517–6780. 20 rooms with bath. Restaurant. AE, MC, V.*

$$ ⊞ **Celal Sultan.** A restored formed town house, which opened as a hotel in 1996, the Celal Sultan has hardwood floors and kilims that give rooms a sense of warmth and quiet sophistication. From the rooftop terrace you can enjoy a fine view of the Blue Mosque and the Sea of Marmara. Unusual for Istanbul, the water in the hotel is filtered. The proprietor, Mr. Selami, and his wife are full of good sightseeing and shopping tips. ⊠ *Salkımsöğüt Sok. 16, Yerebatan Cad., Sultanahmet, 34410,* ☎ *212/520–9323,* FAX *212/522–9724. 19 rooms with bath, 1 suite. Restaurant. MC, V.*

$$ ⊞ **Fehmi Bey.** In a beautifully restored and refurbished old town house just off the Hippodrome is this hotel adorned with owner Fehmi Bey's antiques and kilims. After a long day of sightseeing, the sauna and rooftop terrace bar with views of the old city relax and restore both body and soul. Note that only breakfast is served in the restaurant. ⊠ *Üçler Sok. 15, Sultanahmet, 34440,* ☎ *212/638–9083,* FAX *212/518–1264. 18 rooms with bath. Restaurant, sauna. MC, V.*

$$ ⊞ **Hotel Barin.** Modern, clean, and comfortable, this hotel makes up for in convenience, functionality, and a friendly staff what it lacks in atmosphere. It attracts a large number of business travelers as well as tourists. ⊠ *Fevziye Cad. 7, Şehzadebaşı, 34470,* ☎ *212/513–9100,* FAX *212/526–4440. 65 rooms with bath. Restaurant. AE, MC, V.*

$$ ⊞ **Hotel Zürich.** This 10-story hotel is efficient, well run, and one of the choicer options in the Laleli neighborhood (most other choices are sort of shabby, inexpensive places). The lobby is highly polished, and rooms are bright and carpeted and have little balconies. Ask for one of the higher floors; they're quieter. ⊠ *Harikzadeler Sok. 37, Laleli, 34470,* ☎ *212/512–2350,* FAX *212/526–9731. 132 rooms with bath. Restaurant, 2 bars, nightclub. MC, V.*

$$ ⊞ **İbrahim Paşa Oteli.** In the historic Sultanahmet neighborhood, this French-owned hotel in an exquisitely renovated Ottoman house has a rooftop terrace with glorious views of the Blue Mosque. Though rooms are small and simple, the lobby and bar downstairs, where you can have a wonderful breakfast, are warmly decorated and comfortable. The personable staff ensures a relaxing atmosphere. ✉ *Terzihane Sok. 5, Sultanahmet, 34400,* ☎ *212/518–0394 or 212/518–0395,* 𝖥𝖠𝖷 *212/518–4457. 19 rooms with bath. Bar. MC, V.*

$$ ▥ **Kybele.** Named after an ancient Anatolian fertility goddess, the Kybele has numerous fascinating features, including a lobby lighted by 1,002 lamps, antique furniture, kilims, and calligraphic plates. Rooms have dark-wood furniture and bare walls, and some have kilims. ✉ *Yerebatan Cad. 35, Sultanahmet, 34410,* ☎ *212/511–7766,* 𝖥𝖠𝖷 *212/513–4393. 16 rooms with bath. Restaurant. MC, V.*

$$ ▥ **Pierre Loti.** The tree-shaded terrace café and bar of this little hotel face onto Divan Yolu. The property is centrally located in Old Stamboul, within easy walking distance of most sights. However, some of the rooms have seen better days. ✉ *Piyerloti Cad. 5, Çemberlitaş, 34400,* ☎ *212/518–5700,* 𝖥𝖠𝖷 *212/516–1886. 36 rooms with bath. Restaurant. No credit cards.*

$ ▥ **Alp Guest House.** This small, clean, comfortable hotel in the heart of the old city is run by the Demirbaş family. From the terrace are fine views of the Blue Mosque and the Sea of Marmara. The owners can provide an airport pickup service on request. ✉ *Adliye Sok. 4, Akbıyık Cad., Sultanahmet, 34490,* ☎ *212/517–9570,* 𝖥𝖠𝖷 *212/638–1483. 12 rooms with bath. MC, V.*

$ ▥ **Berk Guest House.** Cheerful Güngör and Nevin Evrensel run this clean, comfortable pansiyon in a converted private home. There are no public spaces to speak of, though two of the rooms have balconies overlooking a garden. ✉ *Kutluğün Sok. 27, Sultanahmet, 34400,* ☎ *212/516–9671,* 𝖥𝖠𝖷 *212/517–7715. 9 rooms with bath. AE, V.*

$ ▥ **Hotel Empress Zoë.** This small, unusual hotel with a
★   friendly staff is near the sights in Sultanahmet. Named for the 11th-century empress who was one of the few women to rule Byzantium, it is decorated in the style of that period. The terrace bar offers fine panoramic views of the old city, and breakfast is served in the garden or indoors. Rooms are accented with colorful textiles and paintings; a couple have terraces and some are very small. Note that to get to the rooms you must climb a spiral staircase. The American owner, Ann Nevans, can help you with your itinerary. ✉ *Akbıyık Cad., Adliye Sok. 10, Sultanahmet, 34400,* ☎

212/518–4360, 𝖥𝖠𝖷 *212/518–5699. 12 rooms with bath, 2 suites. MC, V.*

$ 🏨 **Hotel Nomade.** The service is personal, the beds com-
★   fortable, and the prices low at this Sultanahmet pansiyon. The building is a restored five-story Ottoman house deco-rated with kilims and folk crafts. Rooms are small, and those downstairs share bathroom facilities. The roof-garden bar and terrace have views of Sultanahmet. ⊠ *Ticarethane Sok. 15, Sultanahmet, 34400,* ☎ *212/511–1296 or 212/ 513–8172,* 𝖥𝖠𝖷 *212/513–2404. 16 rooms, some with bath. AE, MC, V.*

Beyoğlu Area

$$$ 🏨 **Galata Residence.** This hotel is in the oldest apartment building in Istanbul, which was built in 1881 for the Ca-mondos, one of the leading banking families of the late Ot-toman Empire. Rooms have been carefully furnished with period furniture, supplemented discreetly with modern conveniences such as bathtubs and air-conditioning. Prices of the one- and two-bedroom apartments, which come with kitchenettes, compare very favorably with rooms at Istanbul's upscale hotels, many of which have only a frac-tion of the Galata's character. Apartments on the upper floors and the top-floor restaurant have excellent views across the Golden Horn to the old city. ⊠ *Felek Sok. 2, Bankalar Cad., Galata, 80020,* ☎ *212/245–0319 or 212/245–0338,* 𝖥𝖠𝖷 *212/244–2323. 16 apartments. Air-conditioning, kitch-enettes, restaurant, café. AE, DC, MC, V.*

$$$ 🏨 **Pera Palace.** Built in 1892 to accommodate guests ar-riving on the *Orient Express,* this hotel is full of atmosphere. Everyone who was anyone in the late 19th and early 20th centuries stayed here, from Mata Hari to numerous heads of state. The rooms once occupied by Kemal Atatürk and Agatha Christie have been turned into museums. The ele-vator looks like a gilded bird cage, the main stairway is white marble, and the lobby surrounding it has 20-ft-high coral-marble walls. Unfortunately, though the hotel has been modernized, its facilities and rooms are not in the greatest shape, making it a hotel for romantics rather than those who need a full range of modern amenities. ⊠ *Meşrutiyet Cad. 98, Tepebaşı, 80050,* ☎ *212/251–4560,* 𝖥𝖠𝖷 *212/*

251–4089. 145 rooms with bath. Restaurant, bar, café. AE, DC, MC, V.

$$ 🏨 **Büyük Londra.** This six-story structure, built in the 1850s as the home of a wealthy Italian family, has grown old gracefully. Rooms are small and comfortably worn, and the current layout has the feel of an old apartment building. The dark woods and velvet drapes used in the high-ceiling lobby and dining room exude an aura of the Ottoman Victorian era. ⊠ *Meşrutiyet Cad. 117, Tepebaşı, 80050,* ☎ *212/293–1619,* ℻ *212/245–0671. 54 rooms with bath. Restaurant. AE, MC, V.*

$$ 🏨 **Richmond Hotel.** On pedestrian İstiklal Caddesi, very close to the consulates, is this hotel in a turn-of-the-century building. Rooms are plush and clean; some have views of the Bosporus. The sidewalk patisserie Lebon at the entrance is a remake of the original. ⊠ *İstiklal Cad. 445, 80070,* ☎ *212/252–5460 or 212/252–9852,* ℻ *212/252–9707. 101 rooms with bath. Restaurant, bar, café, meeting room. AE, V.*

Taksim Square

$$$$ 🏨 **Ceylan Inter-Continental.** Until the mid-1990s, when its lease ran out, this hotel was the Istanbul Sheraton. Extensively refurbished into a plush luxury hotel under its new owners, the Inter-Continental has rapidly become one of Turkey's premier accommodations, with a broad range of top-class facilities. Rooms on the Bosporus side have excellent views. ⊠ *Askerocağı Cad. 1, Taksim, 80200,* ☎ *212/231–2121 or 800/327–0200 in the U.S. or 0345/581–444 in the U.K.,* ℻ *212/231–2180. 390 rooms and 55 suites with bath. 3 restaurants, 3 bars, pool, health club. AE, DC, MC, V.*

$$$$ 🏨 **Hyatt Regency.** This massive but tastefully designed pink building recalls Ottoman splendor. So does the interior, with its plush carpeting and earthy tones. Rooms have views of the Bosporus and the Taksim district. ⊠ *Taşkıla Cad., Taksim, 80900,* ☎ *212/225–7000, 800/228–9000 in the U.S.,* ℻ *212/225–7007. 360 rooms with bath. 3 restaurants, 3 bars, café, pool, beauty salon, Turkish bath, health club, business services, baby-sitting. AE, DC, MC, V.*

$$$$ 🏨 **Istanbul Hilton.** Lavishly decorated with white marble, Turkish rugs, and large brass urns, this is one of the best Hiltons in the chain. The extensive grounds, filled with gardens and rosebushes, make the hotel a restful haven in a bustling city. Rooms are Hilton standard, with plush carpeting and pastel decor; ask for one with a view of the Bosporus. ⊠ *Cumhuriyet Cad., Harbiye, 80200,* ☎ *212/ 231–4650, 800/445–8667 in the U.S.,* 🅵🅰🆇 *212/240–4165. 500 rooms with bath. 4 restaurants, 2 bars, indoor pool, outdoor pool, spa, Turkish bath, 3 tennis courts, health club, squash, shops. AE, DC, MC, V.*

$$$ 🏨 **Divan Hotel.** The staff at this quiet, modern hotel is thoroughly professional. The restaurant is excellent, and the public spaces and good-size rooms are comfortable if a little dowdy. ⊠ *Cumhuriyet Cad. 2, Taksim, 80200,* ☎ *212/231–4100,* 🅵🅰🆇 *212/248–8527. 180 rooms with bath. Restaurant, bar, tea shop, pool. AE, DC, MC.*

The Bosporus

$$$$ 🏨 **Çırağan Palace.** This 19th-century Ottoman palace (pro-
★ nounced *Shi*-rahn) is the city's most luxurious hotel. The setting is exceptional, right on the Bosporus; the outdoor pool is on the water's edge. The public spaces are all done up in cool marble and rich tones. Rooms have Ottoman-inspired wood furnishings and textiles in warm colors (ask for a renovated one); views are exceptional. Most rooms are in the new wing, though there are 12 suites in the palace. ⊠ *Çırağan Cad. 84, Beşiktaş, 80700,* ☎ *212/258– 3377,* 🅵🅰🆇 *212/259–6686. 287 rooms and 28 suites with bath. 4 restaurants, bar, indoor pool, outdoor pool, Turkish bath, putting green, health club. AE, DC, MC, V.*

$$$$ 🏨 **Conrad International Istanbul.** This modern, 14-story tower, catering primarily to business travelers, has spectacular views of the Bosporus and terraced gardens. Rooms are tastefully furnished with all the amenities expected of an international hotel. The staff is congenial and efficient. ⊠ *Barbaros Bul. 46, Beşiktaş, 80700,* ☎ *212/227–3000,* 🅵🅰🆇 *212/259–6667. 620 rooms with bath. 3 restaurants, 2 bars, indoor pool, outdoor pool, 2 tennis courts, health club, shops, business services. AE, DC, MC, V.*

$$$$ ⊡ **Swissôtel Istanbul.** In a superb spot just above
★   Dolmabahçe Palace, this hotel was controversial—nobody
liked the idea of such a big, modern structure towering over
the palace. But you'll appreciate its views—all the way to
Topkapı Palace across the Golden Horn. The vast, high-
ceiling lobby is usually filled with the sound of a tinkling
piano. The occasional Swiss-village mural strikes a jarring
note in Istanbul, but service is crisp and efficient. Rooms,
done in muted greens, have contemporary if undistin-
guished furnishings. ⊠ *Bayıldım Cad. 2, Maçka, 80680,*
☎ *212/259–0101,* ℻ *212/259–0105. 503 rooms with
bath. 7 restaurants, 3 bars, indoor pool, outdoor pool,
health club, business services. AE, DC, MC, V.*

$$$ ⊡ **Büyük Tarabya.** This summer resort, less than an hour's
drive up the Bosporus from the center of Istanbul, is pop-
ular with more affluent locals. Though it has been around
for years, it is well maintained and perfectly modern, with
bright white walls and plenty of cool marble. It has a pri-
vate beach. ⊠ *Kefeliköy Cad., Tarabya,* ☎ *212/262–1000,*
℻ *212/262–2260. 267 rooms with bath. Restaurant, bar,
indoor pool, outdoor pool, health club, beach. AE, MC, V.*

$$ ⊡ **Sed Hotel.** Tucked away on a side street, halfway down
the hill from Taksim Square to Kabataş, the Sed makes up
for being slightly off the tourist track by providing superb
Bosporus views from many of its rooms at half the price
of a five-star hotel. It also has a good restaurant. Insist on
a room with a view. ⊠ *Beşaret Sok. 14, Ayapaşa, 80040,*
☎ *212/252–2710,* ℻ *212/252–4274. 50 rooms with bath.
Restaurant, bar. AE, MC, V.*

5 Nightlife and the Arts

STANBUL'S ARTS AND ENTERTAINMENT OF-
FERINGS run the gamut from jazz dens to
belly dancing. For upcoming events, reviews,
and other information, pick up a copy of *The Guide,* a re-
liable bimonthly English-language publication that has listings of hotels, bars, restaurants, and events, as well as
features about Istanbul. The English-language *Turkish
Daily News* is another good resource.

Nightlife

Bars and Lounges

With views of the Bosporus and a top-notch restaurant next
door, **Bebek Bar** (⊠ Bebek Ambassadeurs Hotel, Cevdet
Paşa Cad. 113, Bebek, ☎ 212/263–3000) attracts a dressed-
up crowd. **Beyoğlu Pub** (⊠ İstiklal Cad. 140/17, Beyoğlu,
☎ 212/252–3842), in a pleasant garden in summer and
indoors in winter, draws moviegoers from nearby theaters
and expatriates. At the opposite end of İstiklal Caddesi from
Taksim Square, **Cafę Gramofon** (⊠ Tünel Meyd., No. 3,
Tünel, ☎ 212/293–0786), a café during the day, becomes
a jazz bar evenings Tuesday–Saturday. At **Cuba Bar** (⊠
Vapur İskelesi Sok. 20, Ortaköy, ☎ 212/260–0550), in the
bohemian Ortaköy district, a band serves up Latin rhythms
while the cook prepares a special Cuban soup and other
dishes.

Hayal Kahvesi (⊠ Büyükparmakkapı Sok. 19, Beyoğlu, ☎
212/224–2558) is a smoky, crowded late-night hangout for
a mostly young crowd that likes live (and loud) rock and
blues. As its name suggests, **Istanblues** (⊠ Tarihi Darphane
Binaları, Topkapı Sarayı, Sultanahmet, ☎ 212/520–5178)
is a blues and jazz bar, open every day from 10 AM to 2 AM,
with live blues and jazz every night except Monday. What
makes it unusual is its location in what was formerly the
Imperial Mint of the Ottoman sultans. **Memo's** (⊠ Salhane
Sok. 10, Ortaköy, ☎ 212/260–8491), on the Bosporus, is
home to an ostentatious crowd; the dancing gets going
around 11 PM.

The **Orient Express Bar** (⊠ Pera Palace Hotel, Meşrutiyet
Cad. 98, ☎ 212/251–4560) is hard to beat for its turn-of-

the-century atmosphere; you can't help but sense the ghosts of the various kings, queens, and Hollywood stars who have passed through its doors. **Roxy** (⊠ Arslanyatağı Sok. 9, Sıraselviler, Taksim, ☎ 212/249–4839) is a popular bar with a spirited, young crowd; it also serves a good range of foods to snack on between drinks and music. Young professionals patronize **Zihni** (⊠ Bronz Sok. 1/A, Teşvikiye, Maçka, ☎ 212/233–9043) for lunch and for evening cocktails. In summer it relocates to a terrace bar on the shores of the Bosporus (⊠ Muallim Naci Cad. 19, Ortaköy, ☎ 212/258–1154).

Dance Clubs

Dance clubs get rolling by about 10 and usually keep going until 3 or 4 in the morning. **Regine's** is described in Nightclubs, *below.* **Club 14** (⊠ Abdülhakhamit Cad. 63, Talimhane, ☎ 212/256–2121) is, as its hours—11 PM to 4 AM—suggest, a lively late-night spot. The classy **Club 29** (⊠ Paşabahçe Yolu, Çubuklu, ☎ 216/322–2829) holds forth in a faux-Roman villa by the Bosporus on the Asian side from mid-June through September. **Millennium** (⊠ Nizamiye Cad. 14, Taksim, ☎ 212/256–4437) is the place to dance and be seen for Istanbul celebrities, wanna-bes, and local gossip columnists. **Şamdan** (⊠ Nisbetiye Cad., Etiler, ☎ 212/263–4898; ⊠ Piyasa Cad. 101, Büyükada, ☎ 216/382–2654 in summer), which also has a fancy restaurant, is favored by fashionable Turks and international expatriates.

Nightclubs

Probably a good deal tamer than you might have expected to find in Istanbul, the city's nightclub shows include everything from folk dancers to jugglers, acrobats, belly dancers, and singers. Some routines are fairly touristy but still fun. Typically, dinner is served after 8, and floor shows start around 10. Be aware that these are not inexpensive once you've totaled up drink, food, and cover. Reservations are a good idea; be sure to specify whether you're coming for dinner as well as the show or just for drinks.

Note that at the seedy striptease places off İstiklal Caddesi, the goal is to get customers to pay outrageous drink prices for questionable companionship. Those unwary enough to enter such places have reported being physically intimidated when questioning a drinks bill that has run into the hundreds of dollars.

Galata Tower (✉ Kuledibi, ☎ 212/245–1160) is high atop the new town in a round room sheathed in windows; the ambience is strictly hotel lounge, and the Turkish dishes are only average. The fixed prices are around $70 for the show and dinner and $40 for the show and a drink. Comfortable, well-established **Kervansaray** (✉ Cumhuriyet Cad. 30, ☎ 212/247–1630) hosts a varied floor show, including two belly dancers, regional folk dances, and medleys of songs from around the world; it serves a variety of Turkish dishes and costs about $70 for the show and dinner, $50 for the show and a drink. **Orient House** (✉ Tiyatro Cad. 27, Eminönü, ☎ 212/517–6163 or 212/517–3488) presents a floor show with belly dancers and Turkish folk dancing, along with good traditional Turkish food. It's about $75 for the show and dinner and $50 for the show and a drink. The revue at **Regine's** (✉ Cumhuriyet Cad. 16, ☎ 212/247–1630) features some of Istanbul's best-known belly dancers, soft-core strippers, and big dance-production numbers; an adjacent upscale disco hops until 4 AM.

The Arts

The **Istanbul International Festival,** held from late June through mid-July, attracts renowned artists performing modern and classical music, ballet, opera, and theater. Shows occur throughout the city in historic buildings, such as Aya Irini and Rumeli Hisar. To order tickets in advance, apply to the ✉ Istanbul Foundation for Culture and Arts (Kültür ve Sanat Concer Vakfi, İstiklal Cad. 146, Beyoğlu, 80070, ☎ 212/293–3133).

In May Istanbul hosts an **International Theater Festival,** which attracts major stage talent from eastern and western Europe. Because there is no central ticket agency, ask your hotel to help you get tickets or inquire at the box office or local tourist offices.

CHASE

Flying to France on Friday? Get Francs from Chase on Thursday. Call Currency To Go at 935-9935 for overnight delivery.

Or pounds for London. Or Deutschmarks for Düsseldorf. Or any of 75 foreign currencies. Call **Chase Currency To Go**SM at **935-9935** in area codes 212, 718, 914, 516 and Rochester, N.Y.; all other area codes call 1-800-935-9935. We'll deliver directly to your door.* Overnight. And there are no exchange fees. Let Chase make your trip an easier one.

CHASE. The right relationship is everything.SM

With guidebooks for every kind of travel—from weekend getaways to island hopping to adventures abroad—it's easy to understand why smart travelers go with **Fodor's**.

At bookstores everywhere.
www.fodors.com

with **Fodor's**™

Concerts

The **Aksanat Cultural Center** (✉ Akbank Bldg., İstiklal Cad., Beyoğlu, ☎ 212/252–3500) shows classical and jazz concerts on a large laser-disc screen, presents films, and hosts exhibitions.

Istanbul's main concert hall is **Atatürk Kültür Merkezi** (☎ 212/251–5600), in Taksim Square. The Istanbul State Symphony performs here from October through May, and ballet and dance companies do shows year-round.

The Touring and Automobile Association (☎ 212/231–4631) organizes chamber music performances at **Beyaz Köşk** (in Emirgan Parkı) and **Hıdiv Kasrı** (in Çubuklu), two small 19th-century palaces. For information contact the association.

The **Cemal Reşit Rey Concert Hall** (✉ Gümüş Sok., Harbiye, ☎ 212/231–5498), close to the Istanbul Hilton, hosts recitals, chamber and symphonic music, modern dance, rock, folk, and jazz concerts performed by international talent. Tickets are often less than half the price they might be in the United States or Europe.

Film

Some theaters on the strip of İstiklal Caddesi between Taksim and Galatasaray show the latest from Hollywood, with a few current European or Turkish movies thrown in. There are also plush, modern theaters at the Istanbul Princess Hotel, in Maslak, and Akmerkez shopping center, in Levent. It's a good idea to purchase tickets in advance for the latter, particularly on weekends. Most foreign films are shown with their original soundtrack and Turkish subtitles, although many children's films are dubbed into Turkish. Look for the words *İngilizce* (English) or *orijinal* (original language). Films in languages other than English will have subtitles in Turkish. When in doubt, ask at the ticket office whether the film is dubbed (*dublaj*) or subtitled (*altyazılı*).

The annual **Istanbul International Film Festival,** which is held in the first two weeks of April, presents films from around the world; ask for a schedule at any box office and make sure to purchase tickets in advance. Seats are reserved.

6 Shopping

I T IS ALMOST IMPOSSIBLE to visit Istanbul without buying something. Whether you're looking for trinkets and souvenirs, kilims and carpets, brass and silverware, leather, old books, prints and maps, or furnishings and clothes (Turkish textiles are among the best in the world), you can find them in Istanbul. Shopping in the city also provides a snapshot of its contrasts and contradictions, from migrants from eastern Turkey selling their wares on the streets to the leisurely, time-honored haggling over endless glasses of tea in bazaars and back alleys to the credit cards and bar codes of the plush, upscale Western-style department stores.

For more about shopping in Istanbul, *see* Essential Information and Pleasures and Pastimes in Chapter 1.

Markets

The **Grand Bazaar** (☞ Chapter 2) is a neighborhood unto itself and a trove of all things Turkish—carpets, brass, copper, jewelry, textiles, and leather goods. The fashions are not bad either—though not quite up to Italian style, they're dramatically less expensive. **Nuruosmaniye Caddesi,** one of the major streets leading to the Grand Bazaar, is lined with some of Istanbul's most stylish shops, with an emphasis on fine carpets, jewelry, and made-in-Turkey fashions. A flea market is held in **Beyazıt Square,** near the Grand Bazaar, every Sunday. In recent years it has become a favorite with street traders from the former Eastern Bloc, who sell everything from cheap vodka and electronic goods to cast-off Red Army uniforms. The **Arasta Bazaar** in Sultanahmet is one of few markets open on Sunday; you can get a lot of the same items here as at the Grand Bazaar and the atmosphere is a lot calmer.

Definitely worth seeing is the **Egyptian Bazaar** (☞ Grand Bazaar to Eminönü *in* Chapter 2), also known as the Spice Market. The **Balıkpazarı** (Fish Market) sells, despite its name, everything connected with food, from picnic supplies to exotic spices and teas; it's on Beyoğlu Caddesi off İstiklal Caddesi. **Sahaflar Çarşışı** is home to a bustling book market, with old and new editions; most are in Turkish, but English and other languages are represented. The market is open daily, though Sunday has the most vendors. Along the Bosporus in the **Ortaköy** neighborhood is a Sunday crafts market with street entertainment.

Shopping Areas

İstiklal Caddesi is a street with everything from stores selling old books and Levis to the Vakko department store to a less stylish Turkish version of Saks Fifth Avenue. The **high-fashion district** centers on Halâskârgazi Caddesi and Rumeli Caddesi in Nişantaşı, 1 km (½ mi) north of İstiklal Caddesi. Here you will find the best efforts of Turkish fashion designers. **Bağdat Caddesi** and **Bahariye Caddesi,** on the Asian side, are the places to find more suburban shopping venues. The **Galleria** mall, in Ataköy near the airport, has more than 100 stores selling foreign and local brand-name clothing. **Akmerkez,** in the Etiler district, is a large and luxurious mall whose stores stock recognized trademarks. The center has a movie theater, a restaurant, a fast-food court, and cafés.

Specialty Stores

Antiques

These are a surprisingly rare commodity in this antique land, perhaps because the government, to ensure that Turkish culture is not sold off to richer nations, has made it illegal to export most categories of antiques more than 100 years old.

Çığır Kitabevi (⊠ Sahaflar Çarşışı 17) has an impressive collection of old books, many of them illustrated. If you know old books, you can pick up bargains from the dozen or so shops at the **Kasımpaşa** flea market (⊠ Kulaksız Cad. 5, Büyük Çarşı, Kasımpaşa); the **Horhor** flea market, in Aksaray (⊠ Kırık Tulumba Sok. 13–22, Aksaray); or, on the Asian side of the city, the **Kadıköy** flea market (⊠ Çakıroğlu İşhanı, Tellalzade Sok., Moda Cad., Kadıköy). **Ory & Ady** (⊠ Serifagu Sok. 7–8, in the bedestan section of the Grand Bazaar) specializes in Ottoman miniatures, illustrations, and prints. **Sofa** (⊠ Nuruosmaniye Cad. 42) stocks a fascinating collection of old maps and prints, original İznik and Kütahya ceramics, vintage jewelry, and assorted other treasures.

Carpets and Kilims

You can find carpet shops at nearly every turn, all stocking rugs for a variety of prices. Each shop has slightly different pieces, so it's best to look at several to get a feel for the market. On the other hand, there's nothing wrong with buying from the first shop you go into if you find something you love.

Some of the better shops in Istanbul include: **Adnan Hassan** (✉ Halıcılar Cad. 90); **Al-Dor** (✉ Faruk Ayanoğlu Cad. 5–8); **Celletin Senghor** (✉ Grand Bazaar); and **Ensar** (✉ Arasta Bazaar 109). Also try the shops along Nuruosmaniye Caddesi, particularly **Çınar,** at Number 6.

Clothing

Angel Leather (✉ Nuruosmaniye Cad. 67) has kidskin suede and leather skirts and jackets; the best of Turkish leather is on a par with Italian leather quality-wise, though the designs are not as stylish. Fashionable **Beymen** (✉ Halâskârgazi Cad. 230) is Istanbul's version of Bloomingdale's. **Beymen Club** (✉ Rumeli Cad. 81 and Akmerkez shopping mall, in Etiler) sells casual Polo-style clothing. **Silk and Cashmere** (✉ Akmerkez shopping mall, in Etiler, or Galleria shopping mall, in Ataköy, or on the Asian side, Carrefour shopping mall, in Kozyatağı) carries a fine selection of high-quality, affordable silk and cashmere menswear and women's wear.

Sube (✉ Arasta Bazaar 131) has handmade kilim slippers with leather soles and kilim boots for a fraction of their prices in the U.S. **Vakko** (✉ İstiklal Cad. 123–125, Beyoğlu or Akmerkez shopping mall, in Etiler, or on the Asian side, Bağdat Cad. 422, in Suadiye) is one of Turkey's oldest and most elegant fashion houses, with an excellent fabric department. President Clinton can occasionally be seen sporting one of the Vakko ties presented to him by visiting Turkish delegates. Turkish designer **Zeki Triko** (✉ Valikonağı Cad.) sells his own bathing suits, completely up-to-date, at his eponymous boutiques.

English-Language Bookstores

Many larger hotels and souvenir shops in the old city stock some English-language newspapers and books, mostly guides to the more famous sights. A more comprehensive range can be found at specialty stores in Beyoğlu and the fashionable shopping districts of Nişantaşı and Levent. Books originally published outside Turkey are marked up 15%–75%.

Some of the larger bookstores carrying English-language books include: **Homer** (⊠ Yeni Çarşı Cad. 28A, Galatasaray, Beyoğlu, ☎ 212/249–5902); **Net** (⊠ Şifa Hamamı Sok. 18/2, Sultanahmet 34410, ☎ 212/516–8467); **Pandora** (⊠ Büyük Parmakkapı Sok. 3, Beyoğlu, ☎ 212/245–1667); **Remzi Kitabevi** (⊠ Akmerkez shopping mall, basement floor, No. 121, Levent, ☎ 212/282–0245; and ⊠ Rumeli Cad. 44, Nişantaşı, ☎ 212/234–5475); and **Robinson Crusoe** (⊠ İstiklal Cad. 389, Tünel, Beyoğlu, ☎ 212/293–6968).

A number of stores specialize in secondhand books, many in English, from dog-eared thrillers to rare old texts about the city. These include: **Aslıhan Sahaflar Çarsısı** (⊠ Galatasaray Balık Pazarı, Beyoğlu); **Librairie de Pera** (⊠ Galip Dede Sok. 22, Tünel, ☎ 212/245–4998); and a cluster of antiquarian booksellers in the **Sahaflar Çarsısı** (⊠ Sahaflar Çarsı Sok., Beyazıt).

Jewelry

The most common types of jewelry you'll see are amber necklaces and ethnic Turkish silver jewelry threaded with coral and lapis lazuli. **Georges Basoğlu** (⊠ Cevahir Bedestan 36–37) and **Venus** (⊠ Kalpakcılar Cad. 160) sell distinctive and original pieces. **Nasit** (⊠ Arasta Bazaar 111) often carries vintage silver jewelry as well as new items. **Urart** (⊠ Abdi İpekçi Cad. 181) has chic interpretations of ancient Anatolian designs.

7 Side Trips from Istanbul

PRINCES ISLANDS

20 km (12 mi) off the coast of Istanbul from Sultanahmet.

The nine islands in the Sea of Marmara have proven a useful amenity for Istanbul. In the days when the city was known as Constantinople, religious undesirables sought refuge here; in the time of the sultans, the islands provided a convenient place to exile untrustworthy hangers-on. By the turn of the last century, well-heeled businessmen had staked their claim and built many of the Victorian gingerbread–style houses that lend the islands their charm. But the islands remained a place of refuge. In the 1930s Büyükada, the largest of the islands, was the home for several years of the exiled Leon Trotsky.

Today the islands provide a leafy retreat from Istanbul. Restrictions on development and a ban on automobiles maintain the old-fashioned peace and quiet—transportation is by horse-drawn carriage or bicycle. Though there are no real sights and populations swell significantly on summer weekends, the Princes Islands are perfect for relaxed outings. Of the nine islands, only four have regular ferry service, and only the two largest, Büyükada and Heybeli, are of real interest. Both are hilly and wooded, and the fresh breeze is gently pine scented.

The price categories in the lodging listings below refer to the price charts in On the Road with Fodor's at the front of this book.

Büyükada

To the left as you leave the ferry, you will see a handful of restaurants with names like Monte Carlo, Capri, and Milano. They are pleasant dives, though somewhat overpriced, and there's little difference among them. **Yörük Ali Plaj,** the public beach on the west side of the island, is an easy walk from the harbor and also has a little restaurant.

To see the island's splendid old Victorian houses, walk to the clock tower and bear right. Carriages are available at the clock tower square. The carriage tour winds up hilly lanes lined with gardens filled with jasmine, mimosa, and imported palm trees. After all of Istanbul's mosques and palaces, the frilly pastel houses come as something of a surprise. But it's quite easy to imagine men in panama hats and women with parasols having picnics out in the garden. You can have your buggy driver wait while you make the 20-minute hike up Yücetepe Hill to the **Greek Monastery of St. George,** where there are three chapels and a sacred fountain believed to have healing waters. As you walk up the path, notice the pieces of cloth, string, and paper that visitors have tied to the bushes and trees in hope of a wish coming true. This is a popular pilgrimage site, especially at Greek Easter, when hundreds take the hike barefoot. If you're lucky, the monastery will be serving its homemade wine.

Dining and Lodging

There is little difference from one spot on Büyükada's restaurant row to the next. The best bet is to look at a menu and ask to see the dishes on display. If a place is crowded with Turks, it is usually good.

$$$ ☒ **Splendid Hotel.** For character, it's hard to beat this wooden turn-of-the-century hotel, with its old-fashioned furniture, large rooms, and Ottoman Victorian styling. The building is topped by twin white domes, copies of those at the Hotel Negresco in Nice. It's difficult to get a room on summer weekends unless you book ahead. ☒ *23 Nisan Cad. 71, Büyükada, 81330,* ☎ *216/382–6950,* ℻ *216/382–6775. 70 rooms with bath. Restaurant, pool. MC, V. Closed Oct.–Apr.*

Heybeli

The big building to the left of the dock, the **Deniz Kuvvetler** (Turkish Naval Academy), is open to visitors every day except Sunday, though there's not really that much to see. To the right of Heybeli's dock are teahouses and cafés stretching along the waterfront. You can take a leisurely carriage ride, stopping, if the mood strikes, at one of the island's several small, sandy, and rarely crowded beaches—the best are on the north shore at the foot of **Değirmen Burnu** (Windmill Point) and **Değirmen Tepesi** (Windmill Hill). You can rent a rowboat for a few dollars at these beaches and row out to one of the other Princes Islands across the way. You will also pass the ruined monastery of the **Panaghia,** founded in the 15th century. Though damaged by fires and earthquakes, the chapel and several red-tile-roofed buildings remain. Carriages here do not climb the hills above the harbor, where the old mansions and gardens are. The walk, however, is not that strenuous.

Lodging

$$$ 🏨 **Merit Halki Palas.** A member of the Merit chain, the Halki Palas was opened in 1994 after its predecessor, which had been built in the 1850s, burned down. But the character of the old hotel has been retained, with white-painted wood, ornate eaves, and large, airy rooms. It's one of the most restful hotels in Istanbul, and though the island has few sights of its own, the old city is only an hour away by ferry. ⊠ *Refah Şehitleri Cad. 88, 81340, Heybeliada,* ☎ *216/351–8890,* 🖷 *216/351–8483. 45 rooms with bath. Restaurant, pool. MC, V.*

Princes Islands Essentials

Arriving and Departing

Ferries (80¢–$1.70) make the trip from Sirkeci or Bostancı (Asian side) docks in half an hour to an hour, depending on where they depart. Go straight to Büyükada and catch a local ferry to Heybeli later. You must pay each way. In summer the early evening ferries returning to the mainland are often very crowded on weekends. Much quicker, though less romantic, is the sea bus, departing from Kabataş near the Dolmabahçe Mosque and from Bostancı sea-bus terminals on the Asian side. Buy tokens for the sea bus at the terminals.

Getting Around

Since no cars are allowed on the islands, you do most of your exploring on foot. Horse-drawn carriage tours cost $10 to $15. The other, perhaps more strenuous but definitely fun, option is to rent a bicycle ($2 per hour) from one of the shops near the clock tower on Büyükada. To get from one of the Princes Islands to the other, hop aboard any of several daily ferries.

EDIRNE

235 km (146 mi) northwest of Istanbul.

Unlike Istanbul, which every conqueror and pretender within marching distance hoped to have as his capital, Thrace was the sort of region that most warriors passed on through. The climate is harsh—sizzling in summer, bitter in winter—and the landscape unexceptional. But the area has some worthy sights, particularly Edirne, founded in the 2nd century AD as Hadrianopolis by the Roman emperor Hadrian. The city has been fought over by Bulgars, crusaders, Turks, Greeks, and Russians through the centuries, though once the Ottoman capital was moved to Istanbul, it became something of a picturesque backwater. The overhanging balconies of traditional Ottoman wooden houses shade Edirne's still-cobbled lanes, and its rich collection of mosques and monuments remains mostly unspoiled by the concrete towers so prevalent in Turkey's boomtowns.

The price categories in the dining and lodging listings below refer to price charts in On the Road with Fodor's at the front of this book.

Hürriyet Meydanı, Edirne's central square, makes a good starting point. Standing in the middle of it is a monument to the city's great passion, wrestling: Two enormous wrestlers steal the spotlight from the obligatory Atatürk statue.

Just off the north side of the Hürriyet Meydanı (Freedom Square) is the **Üç Şerefeli Cami** (Mosque with Three Galleries), built between 1437 and 1447. The galleries circle the tallest of the four minarets, which are notable for their fine brick inlay. On the mosque grounds is the 15th-century **Sokurlu Hamam,** built by Sinan, and one of the country's more elegant baths. It is open to the public from about 8 AM until 10 PM and costs $4 for a bath, $10 for a bath with massage.

Walking east from the square along Talat Paşa Caddesi brings you to the **Eski Cami** (Old Mosque). The mosque is appropriately named: Completed in 1414, it is the city's oldest. The huge-scale calligraphy illustrating quotes from the Koran and naming the prophets is exceptional in its grace and intricacy. Adjoining it is the **Rüstempaşa Ker-**

vansaray (Rüstempaşa Caravansary), restored and reopened as a hotel, just as it was in the 16th century. Also alongside the mosque is the 14-domed **bedestan** (market), and one block away, the **Ali Paşa Bazaar.** Both are more authentic than Istanbul's Grand Bazaar, as the wares sold—coffeepots, kilims, soap shaped like fruits and vegetables, towels—are meant for locals rather than tourists. ⊠ *Talat Paşa Cad., east from Hürriyet Meyd.,* ☎ *no phone.* ☒ *Free.* ☉ *Daily 9–7.*

The other great mosque in Edirne is the striking **Selimiye Cami,** on the outskirts of the city, across the Tunca River. The immense complex is about a 20-minute walk northwest from Hürriyet Meydanı via the fine-hewn, six-arched **Beyazıt Bridge,** which dates from the 1480s, as does the mosque. You can also take a *dolmuş* (shared taxi) from the square. The Selimiye Cami, not Istanbul's Süleymaniye, is the mosque Sinan described as his masterpiece, and it is certainly one of the most beautiful buildings in Turkey. Today a statue of the architect stands in front, but it is hardly necessary; the mosque remains his greatest monument. The architect was 85 years old when it was completed. The central dome, more than 100 ft in diameter and 148 ft high, rests on eight pillars, set into the walls so as not to disturb the interior space. External buttresses help support the weight of 999 windows; legend has it that Sultan Selim thought 1,000 might be a bit greedy. The marble mimber is exquisitely carved, and the mihrab is set back in an apse adorned with exceptional İznik tiles. The *medrese* (mosque compound) houses Edirne's **Türk-Islâm Eserleri Müzesi** (Museum of Turkish and Islamic Art), which displays Islamic calligraphy and photos of local wrestlers, as well as collections of weapons and jewelry from ancient Thrace, folk costumes, kilims, and fine embroidery. ⊠ *Hürriyet Meyd.* ☒ *Free.* ☉ *Daily sunrise–sunset; usually closed to tourists at prayer times, particularly Fri. noon prayers.*

The **Beyazıt Cami** (Beyazıt Mosque) was built by the Sultan Beyazıt, hence its name, at the end of the 15th century. The complex includes both the mosque itself—with a remarkable indented dome and a beautifully fretted mihrab—and two schools, a hospital, a kitchen, and storage depots. Outside the city on the banks of the gently flowing Tunca River, the mosque is rarely used for worship. Apart from visiting tourists or a handful of young boys from the neighboring village playing soccer in the shadow of its walls, the complex is usually deserted by all but the custodian and fluttering pigeons, making it not only one of the most peaceful spots in Edirne but also a poignant reminder of the city's imperial past. ✉ *Head northwest from Hürriyet Meydanı, across Beyazıt Bridge,* ☎ *no phone.* 💰 *Free.* ⊙ *Daily sunrise–sunset during summer; mosque is often locked during winter, but custodian will sometimes open it up.*

Sarayiçi, a field with an arena on one side, is the site of Edirne's famous wrestling tournament. Usually held in June, it is the best known of those held in villages throughout the country: Its burly, olive-oil-coated men have been facing off annually here for more than 600 years. Thousands of spectators turn out. Sarayiçi is a 20-minute walk up the Tunca River from Benazıt Cami.

Dining and Lodging

$ ✕ **Aile Restaurant.** Popular with locals, this restaurant serves stewed meat and vegetable dishes at lunch and switches to grilled fare in the evening. On the second floor above a bank, next to the post office, it is clean and modest and has good, fresh food. ✉ *Belediye Işhanı, Kat 2,* ☎ *284/225–1250. No credit cards.*

$ ✕ **Çatı.** Typical but delicious Turkish dishes are served here, such as *tas kebap* (diced and stewed meat and vegetables with rice or bread) and *islim kebap* (roast lamb covered with strips of eggplant). It's a clean place, if a little shabby, with views of the main square and the market. ✉ *Hürriyet Meyd.,* ☎ *284/225–1307. No credit cards.*

$$ 🏨 **Hotel Rüstem Paşa Kervansaray.** Built in the 1500s, reputedly by the celebrated architect Sinan, today this hotel is the most impressive in Edirne, at least from the outside. The inside is more functional: Rooms have high ceilings and decorative fireplaces, plain furniture, and low, single beds; avoid those near the nightclub, they are noisy. The building sprawls around a pleasant courtyard full of flowers and shaded by a huge plane tree. ✉ *İki Kapılı Han Cad. 57, Sabuni Mah., 22800,* ☎ *284/212–6119 or 284/225–2125,* ℻ *284/212–0462. 100 rooms with bath. Restaurant, nightclub. MC, V.*

$ ⊞ **Açıgöz Oteli.** Modest and nondescript, the Açıgöz Oteli
is efficient, clean, and well located, just off the main square
and opposite the Kervansaray. The hotel does not have the
charm of its neighbor, but its rooms are functional, with all
the basic amenities. A small restaurant serves breakfast but
no midday or evening meals. ⊠ *Tahmis Meyd., Çilingirler
Cad. 9, 22800,* ☎ *284/213–1404 or 284/213–0313,* ℻ *284/
213–4516. 34 rooms with shower. Restaurant. MC, V.*

Edirne Essentials

Arriving and Departing

Buses headed for Edirne depart frequently from Istanbul's
Esenler Terminal. The trip takes four hours and costs $4.
If you're going by **car,** take the toll road—the E80 TEM
(the toll from Istanbul to Edirne costs $3.50), which is
faster and much easier than Route 100. The trip takes
about 2½ hours. Three **trains** leave Istanbul's Sirkeci Station daily for the painfully slow 6- to 10-hour trip; the cost
is about $5, so you are better off taking the bus or driving.

Getting Around

The bus and train stations are on the outskirts of town, too
far to walk. Take a taxi into the center, asking for Hürriyet
Meydanı. Sights in town can all be reached on foot.

Contacts and Resources

Edirne's **tourist information office** (⊠ Talat Paşa Cad., near
Hürriyet Meyd., ☎ 284/213–9208 or 284/225–1518) is open
every day in summer and is generally closed off-season.

TURKISH VOCABULARY

Words and Phrases

	English	Turkish	Pronunciation

Basics

	English	Turkish	Pronunciation
	Yes/no	Evet/hayır	*eh*-vet/*hi*-yer
	Please	Lütfen	*lewt*-fen
	Thank you	Teşekkür ederim	tay-shake-*kur* eh-day-*reem*
	You're welcome	Rica ederim	ree-*jah* eh-day-*reem*
		Bir şey değil	beer shay *day*-eel
	Sorry	Özür dilerim	oh-*zewr* deel-air-eem
	Sorry	Pardon	*pahr*-dohn
	Good morning	Günaydın	goon-eye-*den*
	Good day	İyi günler	ee-yee gewn-*lair*
	Good evening	İyi akşamlar	ee-yee ahk-shahm-*lahr*
	Goodbye	Allahaısmarladık	*allah*-aw-ees-mar-law-deck
		Güle güle	*gew*-leh-*gew*-leh
	Mr. (Sir)	Bay, Bey	by, bay
	Mrs. Miss	Hanım	ha-nem
	Pleased to meet you	Tanıştığımıza memnun oldum	tahnesh-tumu-*zah* *mam*-noon ohl-doom
	How are you?	Nasılsınız?	*nah*-suhl-suh-nuhz

Numbers

	English	Turkish	Pronunciation
	one half	büçük	byoo-*chook*
	one	bir	beer
	two	iki	ee-*kee*
	three	üç	ooch
	four	dört	doort
	five	beş	besh
	six	altı	ahl-tuh
	seven	yedi	yed-dee
	eight	sekiz	sek-*keez*
	nine	dokuz	doh-*kooz*

ten	on	ohn
eleven	onbir	*ohn*-beer
twelve	oniki	*ohn*-ee-kee
thirteen	onüç	*ohn*-ooch
fourteen	ondört	*ohn*-doort
fifteen	onbeş	*ohn*-besh
sixteen	onaltı	*ohn*-ahl-tuh
seventeen	onyedi	*ohn*-yed-dy
eighteen	onsekiz	ohn-sek-*keez*
nineteen	ondokuz	*ohn*-doh-*kooz*
twenty	yirmi	yeer-mee
twenty-one	yirmibir	*yeer*-mee-beer
thirty	otuz	oh-*tooz*
forty	kırk	kerk
fifty	elli	ehl-lee
sixty	altmış	*alt*-muhsh
seventy	yetmiş	*yeht*-meesh
eighty	seksen	sehk-san
ninety	doksan	dohk-*san*
one hundred	yüz	yewz
one thousand	bin	been

Colors

black	siyah	*see*-yah
blue	mavi	*mah*-vee
brown	kahverengi	*kah*-vay-*rain*-gee
green	yeşil	yay-sheel
orange	portakal rengi	poor-tah-kahl rain-gee
red	kırmızı	ker-muz-uh
white	beyaz	*bay*-ahz
yellow	sarı	sah-*ruh*

Days of the Week

Sunday	Pazar	pahz-*ahr*
Monday	Pazartesi	pahz-*ahr*-teh-see
Tuesday	Salı	sahl-luh
Wednesday	Çarşamba	char-shahm-*bah*
Thursday	Perşembe	pair-shem-*beh*

| Friday | Cuma | *joom*-ah |
| Saturday | Cumartesi | joom-*ahr*-teh-see |

Months

January	Ocak	oh-*jahk*
February	Şubat	shoo-*baht*
March	Mart	mart
April	Nisan	nee-*sahn*
May	Mayıs	my-us
June	Haziran	hah-zee-*rahn*
July	Temmuz	*tehm*-mooz
August	Ağustos	ah-oos-tohs
September	Eylül	ey-*lewl*
October	Ekim	eh-*keem*
November	Kasım	kah-suhm
December	Aralık	ah-rah-*luhk*

Useful Phrases

Do you speak English?	Ingilizce biliyor musunuz?	in-*gee-leez*-jay bee-lee-*yohr* moo-soo-nooz
I don't speak Turkish	Türkçe bilmiyorum	*tewrk*-cheh *beel*-mee-yohr-um
I don't understand	Anlamıyorum	ahn-*lah*-muh-yohr-um
I understand	Anlıyorum	ahn-*luh*-yohr-um
I don't know	Bilmiyorum	*beel*-mee-yohr-um
I'm American/	Amerikalıyım	ahm-ay-*ree*-kah-luh-yuhm
I'm British	Ingilizim	*een*-gee-leez-eem
What's your name?	Isminiz nedir?	ees-mee-niz nay-deer
My name is . . .	Benim adım . . .	bay-*neem* ah-duhm
What time is it?	Saat kaç?	sah-aht *kahch*
How?	Nasıl?	*nah*-suhl
When?	Ne zaman?	*nay* zah-mahn
Yesterday	Dün	dewn
Today	Bugün	*boo*-goon
Tomorrow	Yarın	*yah*-ruhn
This morning/ afternoon	Bu sabah/ ögleden sonra	*boo* sah-bah/ *oi-lay*-den sohn-rah

Tonight	Bu gece	*boo* ge-jeh
What?	Efendim?/Ne?	*eh*-fan-deem/neh
What is it?	Nedir?	*neh*-deer
Why?	Neden/Niçin?	*neh*-den/*nee*-chin
Who?	Kim?	keem
Where is . . .	Nerede . . .	*nayr*-deh
. . . the train station?	. . . tren istasyonu?	tee-*rehn* ees-*tah*-syohn-oo
. . . the subway station?	. . . metro durağı?	metro doo-*raw*-uh
. . . the bus stop?	. . . otobüs durağı?	oh-toh-*bewse* dor-*ah*-uh
. . . the terminal? (airport)	. . . hava alanı?	hah-*vah ah*-lah-nuh
. . . the post office?	. . . postane?	post-*ahn*-eh
. . . the bank?	. . . banka?	*bahn*-kah
. . . the hotel?	. . . oteli?	oh-*tel*-lee
. . . the museum?	. . . müzesi?	mew-zay-*see*
. . . the hospital?	. . . hastane?	hahs-*tah*-neh
. . . the elevator?	. . . asansör?	ah-sahn-*sewr*
. . . the telephone?	. . . telefon?	teh-leh-*fohn*
Where are the restrooms?	Tuvalet nerede?	twah-*let* nayr-deh
Here/there	Burası/Orası	*boo*-rah-suh/ *ohr*-rah-suh
Left/right	sağ/sol	sah-ah/sohl
Is it near/far?	Yakın mı?/ Uzak mı?	yah-*kuhn* muh/ ooz-*ahk*muh
I'd like . . .	. . . istiyorum	ees-tee-*yohr*-ruhm
. . . a room	. . . bir oda	beer oh-*dah*
. . . the key	. . . anahtarı	*ahn*-ah-tahr-uh
. . . a newspaper	. . . bir gazete	beer *gahz*-teh
. . . a stamp	. . . pul	pool
I'd like to buy . . .	. . . almak istiyorum	ahl-*mahk* ees-tee-your-ruhm
. . . cigarettes	. . . sigara	see-*gahr*-rah
. . . matches	. . . kibrit	*keeb*-reet
. . . city map	. . . şehir planı	shay-*heer plah*-nuh
. . . road map	. . . karayolları haritası	*kah*-rah-yoh-lahr-*uh* hah-ree-tah-*suh*
. . . magazine	. . . dergi	dair-gee
. . . envelopes	. . . zarf	zahrf
. . . writing paper	. . . mektup kağıdı	*make*-toop *kah*-uh-duh

. . . postcard	. . . kartpostal	cart-poh-stahl
How much is it?	Fiyatı ne kadar?	fee-yaht-uh *neh* kah-dahr
It's expensive/ cheap	pahalı/ucuz	pah-hah-*luh*/ oo-*jooz*
A little/a lot	Az/çok	ahz/choke
More/less	daha çok/daha az	da-ha choke/ da-ha ahz
Enough/too (much)	Yeter/çok fazla	*yay*-tehr/*choke* fahz-lah
I am ill/sick	Hastayım	*hahs*-tah-yum
Call a doctor	Doktor çağırın	dohk-toor *chah*-uh-run
Help!	İmdat!	eem-*daht*
Stop!	Durun!	doo-*roon*

Dining Out

A bottle of . . .	bir şişe . . .	*beer* shee-shay
A cup of . . .	bir fincan . . .	beer *feen*-jahn
A glass of . . .	bir bardak . . .	beer *bar*-dahk
Ashtray	kül tablası	kewl tah-blah-*suh*
Bill/check	hesap	heh-*sahp*
Bread	ekmek	ekmek
Breakfast	kahvaltı	*kah*-vahl-tuh
Butter	tereyağı	tay-*reh*-yah-uh
Cocktail/aperitif	kokteyl, içki	cocktail, *each*-key
Dinner	aksam yemeği	*ahk*-shahm yee-may-ee
Fixed-price menu	fiks menü	feex menu
Fork	çatal	*chah*-tahl
I am a vegetarian/ I don't eat meat	vejeteryenim/ et yemem	vegeterian-*eem*/ eht yeh-*mem*
I cannot eat . . .	. . . yiyemem	yee-yay-mem
I'd like to order . . .	. . . ısmarlamak isterim	us-mahr-lah-*mahk* ee-stair-eem
I'd like . . .	. . . isterim	ee-stair-*em*
I'm hungry/ thirsty	acıktım/ susadım	ah-*juck*-tum/ soo-sah-*dum*
Is service/the tip included?	Servis fiyata dahil mi?	sehr-vees *fee*-yah-tah dah-heel-*mee*
It's good/bad	güzel/güzel değil	gew-*zell*/gew-*zell* day-eel
It's hot/cold	sıcak/soğuk	suh-*jock*/soh-uk
Knife	bıçak	buh-*chahk*

Lunch	öğle yemeği	*oi*-leh *yeh*-may-ee
Menu	menü	meh-*noo*
Napkin	Peçete	*peh*-cheh-teh
Pepper	Karabiber	kah-*rah*-bee-behr
Plate	tabak	tah-bahk
Please give me . . .	Lutfen bana . . . verirmisiniz.	*loot*-fan bah-nah vair-*eer*-mee-see-niz
Salt	tuz	tooz
Spoon	kaşık	kah-*shuhk*

INDEX

X = restaurant, 🏨 = hotel

NOTES

NOTES

With guidebooks for every kind of travel—from weekend getaways to island hopping to adventures abroad—it's easy to understand why smart travelers go with **Fodor's**.

At bookstores everywhere.
www.fodors.com

Smart travelers go with **Fodor's**™

Fodor's Travel Publications

Available at bookstores everywhere. For descriptions of all our titles and a key to Fodor's guidebook series, visit www.fodors.com/books

Gold Guides

U.S.

Alaska
Arizona
Boston
California
Cape Cod,
Martha's Vineyard,
Nantucket
The Carolinas &
Georgia
Chicago
Colorado

Florida
Hawai'i
Las Vegas, Reno,
Tahoe
Los Angeles
Maine, Vermont,
New Hampshire
Maui & Lāna'i
Miami & the Keys
New England
New Orleans

New York City
Oregon
Pacific North
Coast
Philadelphia & the
Pennsylvania
Dutch Country
The Rockies
San Diego
San Francisco

Santa Fe, Taos,
Albuquerque
Seattle &
Vancouver
The South
U.S. & British
Virgin Islands
USA
Virginia &
Maryland
Washington, D.C.

Foreign

Australia
Austria
The Bahamas
Belize &
Guatemala
Bermuda
Canada
Cancún, Cozumel,
Yucatán Peninsula
Caribbean
China
Costa Rica
Cuba
The Czech
Republic &
Slovakia
Denmark

Eastern &
Central Europe
Europe
Florence, Tuscany
& Umbria
France
Germany
Great Britain
Greece
Hong Kong
India
Ireland
Israel
Italy
Japan
London

Madrid &
Barcelona
Mexico
Montréal &
Québec City
Moscow,
St. Petersburg,
Kiev
The Netherlands,
Belgium &
Luxembourg
New Zealand
Norway
Nova Scotia, New
Brunswick, Prince
Edward Island
Paris
Portugal

Provence &
the Riviera
Scandinavia
Scotland
Singapore
South Africa
South America
Southeast Asia
Spain
Sweden
Switzerland
Thailand
Toronto
Turkey
Vienna & the
Danube Valley
Vietnam

Special-Interest Guides

Adventures to
Imagine
Alaska Ports of Call
Ballpark Vacations
The Best Cruises
Caribbean Ports
of Call
The Complete
Guide to America's
National Parks
Europe Ports of Call
Family Adventures
Fodor's Gay Guide
to the USA

Fodor's How to Pack
Great American
Learning Vacations
Great American
Sports & Adventure
Vacations
Great American
Vacations
Great American
Vacations
for Travelers
with Disabilities
Halliday's
New Orleans
Food Explorer

Healthy Escapes
Kodak Guide to
Shooting Great
Travel Pictures
National Parks
and Seashores
of the East
National Parks of
the West
Nights to Imagine
Orlando Like a Pro
Rock & Roll
Traveler Great
Britain and Ireland

Rock & Roll
Traveler USA
Sunday in San
Francisco
Walt Disney
World for Adults
Weekends in
New York
Wendy Perrin's
Secrets Every
Smart Traveler
Should Know
Worlds to Imagine

Fodor's Special Series

Fodor's Best Bed & Breakfasts
America
California
The Mid-Atlantic
New England
The Pacific Northwest
The South
The Southwest
The Upper Great Lakes

Compass American Guides
Alaska
Arizona
Boston
Chicago
Coastal California
Colorado
Florida
Hawai'i
Hollywood
Idaho
Las Vegas
Maine
Manhattan
Minnesota
Montana
New Mexico
New Orleans
Oregon
Pacific Northwest
San Francisco
Santa Fe
South Carolina
South Dakota
Southwest
Texas
Underwater Wonders of the National Parks
Utah
Virginia
Washington
Wine Country
Wisconsin
Wyoming

Citypacks
Amsterdam
Atlanta
Berlin
Boston
Chicago
Florence
Hong Kong
London
Los Angeles
Miami
Montréal
New York City
Paris
Prague
Rome

San Francisco
Sydney
Tokyo
Toronto
Venice
Washington, D.C.

Exploring Guides
Australia
Boston & New England
Britain
California
Canada
Caribbean
China
Costa Rica
Cuba
Egypt
Florence & Tuscany
Florida
France
Germany
Greek Islands
Hawai'i
India
Ireland
Israel
Italy
Japan
London
Mexico
Moscow & St. Petersburg
New York City
Paris
Portugal
Prague
Provence
Rome
San Francisco
Scotland
Singapore & Malaysia
South Africa
Spain
Thailand
Turkey
Venice
Vietnam

Flashmaps
Boston
New York
San Francisco
Washington, D.C.

Fodor's Cityguides
Boston
New York
San Francisco

Fodor's Gay Guides
Amsterdam
Los Angeles & Southern California

New York City
Pacific Northwest
San Francisco and the Bay Area
South Florida
USA

Karen Brown Guides
Austria
California
England B&Bs
England, Wales & Scotland
France B&Bs
France Inns
Germany
Ireland
Italy B&Bs
Italy Inns
Portugal
Spain
Switzerland

Languages for Travelers (Cassette & Phrasebook)
French
German
Italian
Spanish

Mobil Travel Guides
America's Best Hotels & Restaurants
Arizona
California and the West
Florida
Great Lakes
Major Cities
Mid-Atlantic
Northeast
Northwest and Great Plains
Southeast
Southern California
Southwest and South Central

Pocket Guides
Acapulco
Aruba
Atlanta
Barbados
Beijing
Berlin
Budapest
Dublin
Honolulu
Jamaica
London
Mexico City
New York City
Paris

Prague
Puerto Rico
Rome
San Francisco
Savannah & Charleston
Shanghai
Sydney
Washington, D.C.

Rivages Guides
Bed and Breakfasts of Character and Charm in France
Hotels and Country Inns of Character and Charm in France
Hotels and Country Inns of Character and Charm in Italy
Hotels of Character and Charm in Paris
Hotels of Character and Charm in Portugal
Hotels of Character and Charm in Spain
Wines & Vineyards of Character and Charm in France

Short Escapes
Britain
France
Near New York City
New England

Fodor's Sports
Golf Digest's Places to Play (USA)
Golf Digest's Places to Play in the Southeast
Golf Digest's Places to Play in the Southwest
Skiing USA
USA Today The Complete Four Sport Stadium Guide

Fodor's upCLOSE Guides
California
Europe
France
Great Britain
Ireland
Italy
London
Los Angeles
Mexico
New York City
Paris
San Francisco

WHEREVER YOU TRAVEL, *H*ELP IS NEVER FAR AWAY.

From planning your trip to providing travel assistance along the way, American Express® Travel Service Offices are always there to help you do more.

Istanbul

Turk Ekspres (R)
Cumhuriyet Caddesi 47/1
Taksim
(90) (212) 2359500

Turk Ekspres (R)
Conrad Hotel Lobby
Eski Yildiz Caddesi Besiktas
(90) (212) 2270248

Turk Ekspres (R)
Istanbul Hilton Hotel Lobby
Cumhuriyet Caddesi Harbiye
(90) (212) 2410248/9

Turk Ekspres (R)
F. K. Gokay Caddesi Okul S 1/1
Altunizade
(90) (216) 3265510

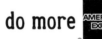

do more AMERICAN EXPRESS

Travel
www.americanexpress.com/travel

**American Express Travel Service Offices
are located throughout Istanbul.**